John G. Gallaher

The Students of Paris

and the Revolution of 1848

Southern Illinois University Press
Carbondale and Edwardsville
Feffer & Simons, Inc.
London and Amsterdam

Copyright © 1980 by Southern Illinois University Press
All rights reserved
Printed in the United States of America
Designed by Richard Neal

Library of Congress Cataloging in Publication Data

Gallaher, John G.
  The students of Paris and the Revolution of 1848.

  Bibliography: p.
  Includes index.
  1. France—History—February Revolution, 1848.
  2. College students—France—Political activity.
  I. Title
  DC270.G314   944.06'3   79-27580
  ISBN 0-8093-0953-X

To My Own Students, Patty, Mike, and Jenny

Contents

Illustrations

Preface

Parisian students have played varying roles in French revolutions over the past one hundred and fifty years. In the summer of 1830, students participated, although not in very large numbers, in the July Revolution, which put an end to the restored Bourbon monarchy and which established the constitutional monarchy of Louis Philippe. In May and June, 1968, the students of Paris were the originators of and principal participants in a "revolution" that nearly brought down Charles de Gaulle and the Fifth Republic. In the years between they took part in many of the significant domestic upheavals that scarred French political life through a monarchy, an empire, and four republics.

In 1848 student participation in the February Revolution, even though it was not massive, was crucial. When a political banquet, organized to protest government policies and scheduled to be held in Paris on February 22, was prohibited by the government, the students and their young allies played a critical role in turning a peaceful crowd that gathered before the church of the Madeleine into a mob that marched on the Chamber of Deputies. Blood was shed when troops dispersed the mob, and barricades, again with the help of students, were erected. Student participation in the three-day revolution was active and meaningful. The manpower for the revolution was provided, as in all French revolutions, by the workers and artisans of the city and nearby suburbs. However, students played important roles not only on the Left

Bank but elsewhere throughout Paris. Medical students cared for the wounded while other students constructed, manned, and even commanded barricades. When the fighting ended the students of the Ecole Polytechnique, many of whom had been energetic during the fighting, rendered valuable assistance to the provisional government in restoring order.

Although they supported the February Revolution, the students were not revolutionaries in the true meaning of the term. Only a relatively small number of those "middle-class" young men were republicans or socialists. They desired changes within the academic community and moderate political reform, but not social or economic upheaval. Thus, when the Parisian workers and artisans again raised barricades in June of the same year for the purpose of bringing about fundamental changes in the social and economic structures of France, the students sided with the government in order to preserve the new status quo.

Of concern here is an analytical evaluation of the condition of the academic community on the eve of the February Revolution of 1848, with special attention to the role played by students in the fall of the monarchy and in the establishment and support of the Second Republic. Also considered is the question of why the students shifted their allegiance to support the government when, in June of the same year, the Parisian workers and artisans once again took to the barricades, despite what has been called a tradition or pattern of friendship with, and support of, the latter and hostility toward the former.

My interest in student participation in revolutions was first aroused in June, 1968, at which time I was living on the Left Bank in Paris and witnessed the last weeks of the "student revolution." However, it was only after discussing those events, and student activism in general in France, with Professor Joseph N. Moody that I undertook this study. I wish to acknowledge further Professor Moody's continual encouragement as this work progressed. I am also indebted to the staff of the National

Archives in Paris and to the chief archivists and their staffs of the Paris police archives and the archives of the Ecole Polytechnique. Without their generous assistance and cooperation this study could not have been completed. Financial assistance from the Office of Research and Projects of the Graduate School of Southern Illinois University at Edwardsville made possible my work in Paris. For this aid I am most grateful.

John G. Gallaher

Edwardsville, Illinois
September, 1979

Introduction

The constitutional monarchy of Louis Philippe came into existence following the July Revolution of 1830, which had driven the last Bourbon king, Charles X, into exile. With its Chamber of Peers, appointed by the king, and its Chamber of Deputies, elected by a very limited suffrage, the regime was a conservative compromise on the part of the influential classes who dominated French political life. The lower classes, in particular the urban workers who had supplied the manpower on the barricades for the July Revolution, derived very few, if any, benefits from the change in government. Within a few years demonstrations and even armed uprisings occurred in Paris and in Lyon as the lower classes attempted to force upon the government the reforms they thought they had won in the summer of 1830.

By 1848 the government of Louis Philippe had outlived the popularity that had ushered it into existence. The king had reigned as a constitutional monarch over a progressively restless population for eighteen years and had cheated an equal number of would-be assassins. "Hardly had I landed at Havre before I heard of the unpopularity of the king and government," wrote Richard Rush, the United States consul to France, in September, 1847. "In Paris, I found this tone increased a hundred-fold. Every voice seemed against the king, as well as leveled against ministers."[1]

Virtually every segment of the population had some grievance against the government. The urban workers, particularly in Paris, where their numbers were concentrated—about 350,000 when families were included—were rapidly developing a class consciousness that had not existed during the Great Revolution of 1789 nor in the summer of 1830. The ideas of Claude-Henri de Rouvroy, count of Saint-Simon, Charles Fourier, Etienne Cabet, and Louis Blanc were being spread by pamphlets, newspapers, secret organizations, and word of mouth. The most popular of these "utopian" socialists was Louis Blanc. His revolutionary concept of the "right to work," which included the plan for what came to be known as "national workshops," was particularly popular in the winter of 1847–48, when France was still struggling to recover from a two-year-old recession.

The general goal of the workers was an improvement in their standard of living, which, translated into more specific terms, meant higher pay, job security, and better working conditions. They looked for little help from the bourgeoisie who controlled the economic life of France. They were gradually coming to the belief that change would have to come through government intervention. In order to influence government they would have to secure the right to vote.

The middle and lower bourgeoisie—the owners of small- and moderate-sized businesses, teachers, many doctors and lawyers, and shopkeepers—the "middle class"—had not been given the right to vote under the July Monarchy. This segment of the population, often educated and of at least moderate means, did not feel that the government, which was dominated by the wealthy bourgeoisie and the nobility, reflected their interests or desires. These interests included greater freedom from government controls and influence in the economic and political life of the nation. To achieve this independence they sought a share in the government, which was translated into a right to vote.

Even within the ranks of the upper classes complete satisfaction with the king's government was not to be found. François Guizot, the historian turned politician, had been the king's chief minister since 1840. His conservative policies, both foreign and domestic, had weakened the limited support he had enjoyed upon coming to power. These policies, coupled with personal rivalries and the ambitions of the members of the "loyal opposition" in the Chamber of Deuputies, created a substantial minority composed of deputies who desired his removal and replacement by a more moderate government controlled by themselves. This "liberal" faction—and the term is used here in comparison with the Guizot government, not with France as a whole—sought a limited extension of the franchise to include the middle bourgeoisie but not the urban workers, the peasants, or even the lower bourgeoisie. Such an extended franchise, they believed, would increase the numbers of the liberal party in the Chamber and would result in their acquisition of power.

The population in rural districts of France, which still accounted for the vast majority of the French citizenry, had little effect upon the events of February, 1848, in Paris. The peasants and the inhabitants of small cities and towns were still oriented toward the land. They were basically conservative socially, economically, and politically. Catholicism was still deeply entrenched outside the principal cities. In the most rural departments of central and western France the old aristocracy remained predominant and provided political, social, and, in some districts, economic guidance. Rural France had little or no understanding of the many problems that plagued Paris and the other large cities as the result of the economic and social changes brought about by new technology. This lack of understanding led to a lack of sympathy for the urban population, and in June, when barricades went up to overthrow the Provisional Government of the Second Republic, rural France opposed them.

The unpopularity of the king and his government was rooted in a variety of causes; however, on some issues, both foreign and domestic, a considerable majority of the French populace could agree. The king's dedication to peace may well have found favor in international quarters and with the upper bourgeoisie at home, but it was not popular with the French people. Guizot summed it up very accurately when he said, "While other nations hate war, France actually likes it. It is an amusement she is sometimes forced to refuse herself, but it is always with regret. Peaceful policy is called—and in one sense *is*—anti-national."[2] Too many had forgotten, or had never known, the suffering and anguish of the Napoleonic Wars, and they dwelt upon the glory of the Empire. It was Austerlitz, Jena, Marengo, and French domination of the Continent that they thought of and not the disastrous retreat from Moscow, or the battles of Leipzig and Waterloo. That the power and influence of France in European and world affairs had diminished during the first half of the nineteenth century was regretted and renounced by French citizens from every walk of life. The government may have desired peace, but France preferred "honor" and "glory."

The recession that had gripped the nation since 1846 had started in the rural districts with poor harvests and had then spread to the industrial towns and cities. Although the recession had adverse effects upon virtually every phase of French economic life, the poor suffered most. The government was unwilling to take any action that would interfere with the free play of the economy as the concept of laissez-faire was still an intricate part of French economic thought. Severe criticism was leveled against the king and his ministers by those whose standard of living was adversely affected. There was a general feeling on the part of the French, naïve perhaps, that if they had a voice in choosing those who governed the nation their economic and social conditions would improve. As only about one out of every thirty adult male citizens was eligible to vote, it was only natural that their rallying point was the right to vote.

Despite these conditions throughout France, no serious or immediate danger to the government was apparent as the year 1847 drew to a close, or even in the early weeks of 1848. The king felt secure enough upon his throne in late December to criticize the liberal opposition when he addressed the Chamber of Deputies on the occasion of the opening of its new session. "In the middle of the agitation," said Louis Philippe, referring to the reform campaign of the political opposition, "which blind or hostile passions are fermenting, one conviction upholds me: it is that we possess in the constitutional monarchy the most certain means for satisfying for everyone the moral and material interests of our dear country."[3] Less than one week before the barricades of February were constructed, Richard Rush dined with the royal family and members of the cabinet at the Tuileries and wrote the following account of the evening to James Buchanan:

I was at the Tuileries on the evening of Saturday the 19th of February. It was an evening when the King received in his customary way, members of the diplomatic corps. . . . The scene was one of tranquility throughout the Palace. On no occasion had I beheld it more so. The Queen was in the room at her usual seat, occupied occasionally at her pastime in embroidery. Most of the royal family were present. The King in conversation with me, alluded to the pending banquet in Paris, which then had not been forbidden, but was in the course of being watched. He said there was no cause of uneasiness and that order would be maintained. No thought of insecurity could have been in his mind.[4]

Count Duchatel (Charles-Marie Tanneguy), who was minister of the interior, expressed complete confidence that the government was in no serious danger just a few days before the revolution toppled the regime. He assured Alexis de Tocqueville, a member of the opposition faction in the Chamber of Deputies, that the government's position was both right and just, and that if it should ever come to fighting—which the government did not desire—the military preparations for the defense of the city of Paris were more than adequate.[5]

Amid this complacency there was at least one who prophesied the February Days. Alexis de Tocqueville, in a speech before the Chamber of Deputies on January 27, 1848,[6] warned of pending revolution in the following words:

It is said that there is no danger because there is no riot, and that because there is no visible disorder on the surface of society, we are far from revolution.

Gentlemen, allow me to say that I think you are mistaken. True, there is no actual disorder, but disorder has penetrated far into men's minds. . . .

Gentlemen, my profound conviction is that we are lulling ourselves to sleep over an active volcano. . . .

I was saying just now that sooner or later (I do not know when or whence) this ill will bring into the land revolutions of the utmost seriousness: be assured that that is so. . . . Do you not feel—how should I say it—a revolutionary wind in the air?[7]

Despite Tocqueville's elegant words Paris was taken very much by surprise when the barricades went up in February.

The student population of France shared the nation's general discontent and added to it the particular grievances of the academic community. The most serious of these grievances were government interference and censorship. Such action on the part of the government might take the form of canceling a course of study that the Ministry of Education found objectionable or of removing a teacher who would not conform to the ministry's code of acceptable behavior. At another time it could be the silencing of a teacher or the refusal to hire a teacher. And at still another time it would be dictating the content of a course. But whatever its form, the students—and in most incidences the faculty as well—found this censorship and interference to be oppressive, and they frequently displayed their opposition.

The Students of Paris
and the Revolution of 1848

.I.

Background for a Revolution

In the early nineteenth century the academic community in Paris comprised the students and faculties of the university, the *grandes écoles* (Polytechnique, Normale, Saint-Cyr, Forestière, and Navale), and those colleges which were not a part of the university. The Collège de France was in a unique position. Officially it was part of the University of Paris, but it functioned virtually independent of the university and had no students of its own. The faculties of the university and of the *grandes écoles* were the best paid in the nation. Positions at these schools were sought for the prestige connected with them as well as for the privilege of residing in the cultural and intellectual center of France. The appointment of faculty was the function of the Ministry of Education. Assignments were made at the end of each academic year.

The secondary schools were the backbone of the French educational system. There were two types of secondary schools during the July Monarchy: The *collège royal* (The *lycée* under the Empire) and the *collège communal*. The principal difference between the two types of schools was that the *collège royal* perpetuated the classical education of the prerevolutionary period with its emphasis on Latin, philosophy, history, and the classics. It was also better funded than the *collège communal*. The *collège royaux*, of which there were forty-six in 1842, were supported and controlled by the central government. The *collèges communals* somewhat de-emphasized Latin, philosophy, and the classics and expanded the curriculum in the sciences and mathematics. They were supported at the department level although their direction was largely in the hands of the national educational bureaucracy. The *collèges royaux* were more prestigious for both students and faculty. Education in these schools was of a higher quality than in the *collèges communals,* and the teachers were better prepared and better paid. Although practically all secondary schools under the constitutional monarchy were housed in ecclesiastical buildings inherited from the *ancien régime,* the *collèges royaux* generally had superior facilities and attracted the more affluent and better prepared students.[1]

There also existed private schools, most of them operated by the Catholic Church. The "seminary" schools on the secondary level were officially meant to serve as preparatory schools for the Catholic clergy; but in practice they comprised an educational system that operated parallel to the state-supported, and -controlled, public schools. During the 1830s and 1840s an increasing number who were graduated from these seminaries chose not to enter the priesthood. In point of fact, many of them never had intended to follow the religious life. The private schools were handicapped by government restrictions, notably those of the Ordinance of 1828, and all efforts to eliminate them under the July Monarchy were frustrated.

The University of Paris comprised a number of semi-independent units called faculties, or schools. The three "higher" faculties were law, medicine, and philosophy. The first two were very popular and flourished in the first half of the nineteenth century. Philosophy had begun to decline in the prerevolutionary days, and although it was still academically prestigious in 1848 it was by far the smallest of the schools numerically. The faculty of arts was made up of a number of *collèges royaux,* the best known of them being Louis-le-Grand.[2] The *collèges* prepared the young men for the baccalaureate, which was required for entrance into a higher school of the university.

The baccalaureate was also required for entrance into

the *grandes écoles,* which were in no way connected with the university. Each of these schools was an independent institution under the supervision of the Ministry of Education; entrance was both limited and selective and was subject to political influence. The most prestigious of the *grandes écoles* were the Ecole Polytechnique and the Ecole Normale.

The physical conditions of the Paris schools ranged from bad to miserable. Almost no buildings for secondary or higher education had been constructed in the capital since the government had taken over responsibility for education in the early years of the Great Revolution. Thus the buildings in use in 1848 were schools and monasteries that the Catholic church had constructed under the *ancien régime.* Most of them were over one hundred years old, with some dating back into the seventeenth century or earlier. Furthermore, little had been done in the way of upkeep or modernization. The lighting, heating, and ventilation were poor according to standards of the mid-nineteenth century.

In direct contrast to the neglected stones and morter of the schools of Paris, the various faculties were staffed, by and large, with the ablest men who could be found. The city was best known for its medical education during the first half of the century. Young men flocked to its lecture halls and hospitals from all over the world.[3] Each time a vacancy occurred on one of the faculties of the university or in one of the *collèges royaux,* the Ministry of Education was flooded with requests and applications. The final selection was made with several considerations in mind. The scholastic ability of a candidate was important, but it was not the sole criterion for appointment. There were also political and sometimes even religious considerations in faculty appointments.[4]

The life of a scholar and teacher in mid-nineteenth-century Paris was still affected by the medieval monastic traditions that had dominated the prerevolutionary university. The most stubborn of these traditions were lodging within the school, the common table, celibacy, and the robe. These practices were stronger in the provinces than in Paris, and in the capital they were more prevalent in the *collèges* than in the faculties of the university. In the *collèges* of Paris and in the *grandes écoles* a substantial minority continued to live within the walls of the schools and to take their meals together. These practices were less common among the professors of the faculties of philosophy, law and medicine. The tradition of celibacy was also declining; yet, in 1842, 58.6 percent of the secondary teachers in France were single.[5] French professors were abandoning the academic robe in such numbers, however, that in 1838 the school administration found it necessary to order them to wear their robes at all times when teaching or taking part in academic functions.

Many members of the faculties of Paris began their teaching careers, and indeed spent many years, in the provinces. Furthermore, the vast majority of them had their origins in provincial towns or cities. The teaching profession, in general, derived its principal strength from the ranks of the middle and the lower bourgeoisie.[6] It might also be noted that, whereas dynasties were not uncommon among magistrates and in the liberal professions, they were rare in the university. Seldom did the sons of professors enter the field of teaching.[7] Their failure to do so may be explained in part by the fact that the pay in the teaching profession was poor. Even though the professors in Paris were better paid than their counterparts in the provinces, their income was not in keeping with either their intellectual level or the years spent in preparation and research.

Government surveillance and control of the teaching corps was another fact of life under the July Monarchy. The obligations of the university corps were spelled out in detail under the Empire in the decrees of March 17, 1808, and November 15, 1811: obedience to the hierarchy, political and religious submission to the wishes of the government, and a sense of duty toward students and colleagues.[8] Each successive government confirmed the decrees. It is true that during the July Monarchy both surveillance and control were more lax than under the

Empire and during the Bourbon Restoration; nevertheless, neither faculty, students, nor administrators were free from supervision and reprisal on the part of the royal administration.

The socioeconomic background of the Parisian student body in the mid-nineteenth century was bourgeois, with the majority of the students coming from families of the middle bourgeoisie: notaries, judges, doctors, proprietors (landlords), and *cadres choyés du pays l*égal ("the coddled ranks of the *pays légal*"). The military aristocracy, and the aristocracy in general, began to abandon the universities and public education as a whole after 1815. This trend continued during the Restoration and was accelerated under the July Monarchy. Nor did the upper bourgeoisie take advantage of the educational opportunities of the university. Both of these segments of society preferred the confessional schools, which flourished in the three decades prior to 1848. The lower bourgeoisie — the *petits fonctionnaires, commercants,* and artisans — was eager for its children to acquire a professional education that would lead to greater wealth and social prestige than its own generation had enjoyed. Law, medicine, high position in the civil service — even a career in teaching — were all considered a step up the social and economic ladders, and in some cases a major step up. Only a limited number among the lower bourgeoisie could afford the relatively high cost of secondary education or a university degree, but their presence was being felt in increasing numbers. Paris, because of its excellent *collèges* and its university, offered greater opportunity to its lower bourgeoisie than did the provinces, though other principal educational centers, such as Strasbourg, Lyon, and Montpellier, did offer substantial opportunities. A boy might live at home and attend school at a minimum cost to his family. Even so, only a small proportion from this relatively numerous segment of the urban population of France attended the university. From the ranks of the moderately well-to-do peasantry, which constituted a small percentage of the population, some students entered secondary and higher schools. By the middle of the century the peasantry was not indifferent to education. Its children were attending elementary schools in steadily increasing numbers, and some were even going on to the *collège communal.* However, only a very small percentage of the students at the university originated from peasant stock.[9]

Among the various *collèges* of Paris were social differences. The Collège Charlemagne, located on the Right Bank between the Hôtel de Ville and the Place des Vosges, attracted the lower bourgeoisie of the Marais. The Collège Bonaparte recruited its students from the *bourgeoisie d'affaires de la Chaussée-d'Antin,* while both the Collège Louis-le-Grand and the Collège Henri IV were patronized by the *bourgeoisie de l'intelligence.* The sons of Louis Philippe and of his chief minister, François Guizot, were educated at Louis-le-Grand. However, their example influenced chiefly the Orleanist bourgeoisie of the capital. The Catholic bourgeoisie in general preferred the confessional schools.

During the course of the nineteenth century there was a clear evolutionary trend toward democratization of the *lycées* and the *collèges* of France. Under the First Empire their students came primarily from the families of the military and from the lower nobility. During the Bourbon Restoration and the July Monarchy the nobility deserted the public schools for private schools and the bourgeoisie became dominant. By the end of the century the impact of the lower bourgeoisie was being felt as a major force.

The life of the student attending the *collège* was totally different from that of a student attending the university. The French even had two different words for the English word *student.* Those young men and boys who attended the *collèges* were referred to as *élèves* (perhaps closer to the infrequently used English term *pupils*) while the term *étudiant* was used for the young men at the university. The great majority of the students attending the *collèges* — *les élèves* — lived in dormitories within the walls of the school. Every aspect of the student's life was regulated and supervised. Students were not allowed to leave the school without permission. With the exception of family emergencies, the young men were given permission to go out into the city on only one afternoon during the week and on Sunday. Unlike the superior schools, attendance at classes was mandatory. Meals were taken in common at prescribed hours. The times for rising and retiring were fixed and uniform. The students passed through the corridors from one class to another in silence and in the classroom they spoke only when addressed. Discipline was severe; punishment was quick and harsh.

The strict way of life in the *collège* was, in part, left over from the prerevolutionary era when the schools were governed by semimonastic regulation; in part, from the military tradition of the *lycées* during the Empire; and, in part, from the mid-nineteenth century bourgeois philosophy that the schools, besides imparting knowledge to their students, were also to prepare them to take their place in a world filled with temptations, dangers, and pitfalls. To cope with such a life, it was asserted, a young man must be taught self-discipline, self-denial, and self-sacrifice. The strict discipline of the *collèges* incited resistance in some students, who reacted impudently and were punished. The vast majority, however, silently bore their unhappy lot and waited for the day when they would be set free.

The following description of the *collège* student has been left by Albert Vandam, an Englishman who lived in Paris during the 1840s:

The collegian wore a top hat, like our Eton boys, a white necktie, a kind of black quaker coat with a stand-up collar, a very dark blue waist coat and trousers, low shoes, and blue woollen stockings. . . . They were virtually prisoners within the walls of the college all the week, for in their Thursday promenades they were little more than prisoners taking exercise under the supervision of their gaolers. They were allowed to leave on alternate Sundays, provided they had parents, relations, or friends in Paris, who could come themselves or send their servants to fetch them in the morning and take them back at night. The rule applied to all, whether they were nine or double that number of years: it prevails even now. I only set foot in a

French college of those days twice to see a young friend of mine,
and I thanked my stars that four or five years of that existence
had been spared to me. The food and table appointments, the
bedrooms — they were more like cells with their barred
windows — would have been declined by the meanest English
servant, certainly by the meanest French one. I have never met
with a Frenchman who looks back with fond remembrance on
his schooldays.[10]

Not all of the students who attended the *collèges* lived
within its confines. There were also "externs," students
who lived with their families or relatives. Living at home
was more common in Paris than in the provinces, but was
to be found throughout France. Those young men who
did so were subject to the same regulations and discipline
as were the "interns" during school hours; however, at
other times they were under parental direction. During
the February Days of 1848 it was the externs who brought
news to their fellow students within the walls of the Parisian *collèges*. It was also from the ranks of the externs that
student participation in the revolution of 1848 at the
collège level was drawn.

Conditions in the *grandes écoles* more closely resembled
those in the *collèges* than those in the superior schools of
the university. The military academy of Saint-Cyr, just
outside Paris, was not unlike England's Sandhurst or the
United States' West Point. Dating from the First Empire
but with its roots in the Ecole Royale Militaire of Paris, it
was already steeped in tradition by 1848. Its students
were drawn from the military families of the period and
from the Orleanist nobility, both of which were firmly
attached to the constitutional monarchy. The school fur-
nished the military elite for the French army and in
return was favored by the government. It is not surpris-
ing that these cadets did not take part in the overthrow of
the monarchy. Rather, it might be asked why they did not
raise a hand to support Louis Philippe.

The Ecole Polytechnique had been founded in 1794 by
the revolutionary government to educate young men
along the more practical and technical lines of the sciences in contrast to the traditionally humanistic educa-

tion of the university. Under Napoleon it experienced a "second founding" and became primarily an engineering school to fulfill the needs of the French army. The emperor also introduced military training and discipline. In this period nearly all its graduates went directly into military service. Under the Bourbon Restoration the *polytechniciens* were disarmed because of their pro-Bonapartism, and the curriculum was gradually revised. By 1848 it was no longer an engineering school in the strictest sense of the term, although its students were still exposed to much mathematics and science. The students still wore uniforms, and discipline was of military nature. The head, or commander, of the school was an army officer and many of the school's practices and traditions were militaristic. The school and its students were supported by the government, and appointments to the institution were made by the government. All students were treated alike. They lived within the walls of the school on the Left Bank and, like the young men in the *collèges,* were allowed out only on Sunday and Thursday. The prescribed course of study at the Ecole Polytechnique enabled the student to complete his studies in two years.

Student life on the eve of the revolution of 1848 varied greatly from the *collèges* and the *grandes écoles* to the faculties of letters, law, and medicine. The students who attended the schools of letters, law, and medicine lived either at home or in rented quarters. They were free of university supervision except when attending classes or school functions. The financial situations of their families governed their styles of life. The room or rooms they occupied, their meals, and their entertainment all depended on their parents' ability to pay.

Albert Vandam, who had an unusually keen awareness of life on the Left Bank in the 1840s, wrote the following:

Paris became to a certain extent, and not altogether voluntarily, cosmopolitan before the palatial mansions, the broad avenues, the handsome public squares . . . excited the admiration of the civilized world. . . . But during the whole of the forties, and even later, the *rive gauche,* with its Quartier-Latin and adjacent Faubourg St. Germain, were almost entirely sacred from the desecrating stare of the deliberate sightseer; and consequently, the former especially, preserved its individuality, not only materially, but mentally and morally—immorally would perhaps have been the word that would have risen to the lips of the observer who lacked the time and inclination to study the life led there deeper than it appeared merely on the surface. For though there was a good deal of roystering and practical joking, and short-lasted *liaison,* there was little of deliberate vice, of strategic libertinism—if I may be allowed to coin the expression. True, every Jack had his Jill, but, as a rule, it was Jill who had set the ball rolling. . . .[11]

There were few [students] whose allowance exceeded two hundred francs per month. A great many had to do with less. Those who were in receipt of five hundred francs—perhaps not two score among the whole number—were scarcely considered as belonging to the fraternity. They were called "ultrapontins," to distinguish them from those who from one year's end to another never crossed the river, except perhaps to go to one of the theatres. . . .

When they [students] were not disporting themselves at Bobino [Bobinot], they were at the Chaumière, and not in the evening only. Notwithstanding the enthusiastic and glowing descriptions of it that have appeared in later days, the place was simple enough. There was a primitive shooting-gallery, a skittle-alley, and so forth, and it was open all day. The students, after having attended the lectures and taken a stroll in the gardens of the Luxembourg, repaired to the Chaumière, where, in fine weather, they were sure to find their "ladyloves" sitting at work demurely under the trees. The refreshments were cheap, and one spent one's time until the dinner hour, chatting, singing, or strolling about. The students were very clannish, and invariably remained in their own sets at the Chaumière. There were tables exclusively occupied by Bourguignons, Angevins, etc. In fact, life was altogether much simpler and more individual than it became later on.[12]

An American student in Paris in 1847–48, Charles Godfrey Leland, also wrote of Bobinot, "a very small theatre in the Quarter-Latin, frequented entirely by students and grisettes."[13] He further described how the students, when they had money, would eat at Magny's, where they paid ten francs for a fine meal, but "When *au sec* [broke], I fed at Flictoleau's—we called him *l'empoisonneur* [the poisoner]—where hundreds of students got a meal of three courses with half a bottle of [wine] *ordinaire,* and not so bad, either, for thirty sous."[14] Considering that the average daily wage of a Parisian worker was 3.80 francs and that 30 percent of all workers in the city earned between 3 and 5 francs per day, the students clearly lived above the poverty level.

The rigid discipline and the restricted life of the students at the *collèges,* which was even worse in the provinces than in Paris, created pent-up aggression and emotions that were later released when the students went on to the higher schools of the university. No longer under the stern, watchful eyes of their supervisors, they used every opportunity to exert their independence and display their newly gained freedom. Their rebellion against authority tended to take the form of opposition to the government, which they expressed in street manifestations and demonstrations.

The curriculum of the schools of France, on every level, was in a constant state of change throughout the first half of the nineteenth century. The basic plan for education at all levels was spelled out in detail by a decree of 1802, and both the Bourbon Restoration and the July Monarchy reaffirmed the decree—with modifications. Scarcely a year went by in which the Ministry of Education did not introduce changes in the curriculum. The basic trends were to increase the amount of science (including mathematics) and social science and to deemphasize the classics and philosophy. One aspect of the struggle was over the Latin requirement for university degees. Another was over the introduction of new branches of science and new degree programs. Faculties split along lines that might be categorized as traditional (classical) and progressive (scientific), and, at times, the fighting became both personal and bitter. Slowly, but steadily, throughout the nineteenth century, the curriculum was "modernized," though not without considerable opposition.[15]

The principal teaching technique in the mid-nineteenth-century university was the formal lecture delivered by a professor, particularly in the higher schools of the university. A faculty member who held a chair in literature, history, or philosophy would give a series of lectures, usually two per week, on a given topic.

The strict control exercised by the government over virtually every aspect of French education inevitably led to friction between the students and the government. Protests were usually mild, orderly, and nonviolent, and the government paid them little heed. Yet the students would, from time to time, mount a major demonstration that would lead to vandalism in the Latin Quarter, or, in alliance with the workers and artisans on the Left Bank, full-scale rioting and even rebellion. The student dissatisfaction directed against the July Monarchy was both of an academic and of a political nature. The students resented the close censorship the government exercised over the faculty and the course content, which censorship *occasionally* took the form of suppression not only for political reasons but also on religious and moral grounds.

The courses of Edgar Quinet and Jules Michelet at the Collège de France were canceled by orders of the government because of their attacks upon religion and, to a lesser extent, for political reasons. Adam Mickiewicz, the well-known Polish poet, lost his position in the same institution because of his political and religious activities. All three professors were popular with the students and, in each incident, the action taken by the ministry aroused antigovernment feelings among the student population of the capital. The canceling of Michelet's course, coming as it did on the eve of the February Revolution, had a direct effect on student attitudes and actions. A brief look at these three affairs will give substantial insight into student feelings at the beginning of the turbulent year.

The first of the three professors to be fired from his post was Adam Mickiewicz. A Polish nationalist in the 1820s, his fiercely nationalistic poetry made it necessary for him to flee his beloved native land. He eventually settled in Paris where in 1840 he held the chair of Slavic literature at the Collège de France. He quickly became the symbol of Polish nationalism and the champion of a free Polish state. His popularity with the students of Paris, who loudly proclaimed their sympathy for the oppressed Poles, was immediate and immense; students flocked to his lectures in ever-increasing numbers. But Mickiewicz did not restrict himself to Polish or even to Slavic affairs, which the French government would, no doubt, have continued to tolerate. He became an active and outspoken Bonapartist and critic of the Catholic church. In his lectures he devoted less time to Slavic literature and more time to politics and religious matters until the Guizot government deprived him of his chair at the Collège. There were manifestations on the part of the students in the capital protesting his dismissal, but they were peaceful and moderate, and the government completely ignored them.

The conflict that arose between Edgar Quinet and the established order caused even greater concern and conflict between the university community and the government. Quinet, born in Bourg in 1803, received a fine education, which included extensive travel throughout Europe and years of study in Germany and Italy. In 1838 Narcisse-Achille de Salvandy, minister of education, appointed him to the chair of literature at the University of Lyon. The relatively young Quinet quickly became as popular a lecturer as he was a poet and author. In less than three years he was given a chair at the Collège de France. His popularity in Paris was almost instantaneous. The university students flocked to his classes. Quinet did not digress in his lectures to the extent that Mickiewicz had done before him, but his attacks on the Catholic church and his obvious sympathy for democracy led to conflict with the government.

From an early age Quinet had looked upon the era of the French Revolution as the apex of the nation's long historical development. He welcomed the overthrow of the Bourbons in 1830. Upon his return from Italy late in the summer of that same year he was overjoyed at the sight of the Tricolor once again flying over France. However, he soon realized that the revolutionary flag did not hail a republic. He was not a revolutionary himself, nor was he even active in politics; but his political preferences were well to the left of the Bourgeois Monarchy, and he sympathized with the moderate political reforms advocated by the parliamentary opposition. On the question of religion it was a different matter. Quinet became a bitter enemy of the Catholic church and, in particular, of the Jesuits. It was his continual vociferous attacks, both in the classroom and through the press, against the church, and to a lesser extent his republicanism, that led the government of François Guizot to strip him of his chair at the Collège de France.

Guizot, who dominated the government from 1840 until he was forced from office by the events of February, 1848, considered the teachings of Edgar Quinet "revolutionary." In 1845 Quinet attacked Catholicism as being incompatible with modern ideas, and he pressed for an immediate separation of church and state and for the unilateral denunciation of the Concordat of 1801, which Napoleon had signed with Pope Pius VII and which still regulated church-state affairs. The government, through the minister of education, Salvandy, attempted to silence the professor. On July 13, 1845, the faculty of the Collège de France voted seventeen to seven in favor of a motion stating that Quinet and Jules Michelet, who was also engaged in attacks upon the church and the government, had not violated the principles of academic freedom and that the collège approved of their teachings. Following this triumph the students of Paris held a large demonstration in honor of the two professors and they even invoked the memory of Mickiewicz. But neither the vote of the faculty nor the enthusiasm of the students was sufficient to save Quinet. By the end of the year his course had been canceled by order of Salvandy. Once again the students moved into the streets, but this time not in triumph. The manifestation was loud but orderly. The students denounced the stifling of academic freedom and demanded Quinet's reinstatement. Their marches, speeches, and shouts had no effect upon the government and the students were forced to content themselves with the fact that at least they still had Michelet.[16]

Jules Michelet had weathered the wrath of the government in 1845 only to follow in the footsteps of Mickiewicz and Quinet in less than three years. Educated in Paris at the Collège Charlemagne, he began his teaching career in 1821 at the Collège Rollin and quickly gained a reputation as a historian. In 1827 he was named *maître de conférences* at the Ecole Normale, and following the revolution of 1830 he succeeded Guizot, also a historian, on the faculty of letters at the University of Paris. Then in 1838 he was named to the chair of history and morals at the Collège de France. Already popular with the students in the capital, Michelet's influence and fame spread through the land as the early volumes of his *History of France* began to appear after 1833. Like Mickiewicz and Quinet, Michelet developed interests in contemporary politics and religion. His attacks upon the Catholic church and the Jesuits, although not as extreme as those of his two contemporaries, caused the government concern and placed his teaching career in jeopardy by 1845. But it was his republicanism that finally brought the Guizot government to the drastic decision that he too must be silenced.

The occasion that presented itself was Michelet's new course. In his first two lectures (delivered in the last weeks of December, 1847) he accelerated his attack on the church. This led to the cancellation of the course on January 2, 1848, on charges that it was an "anachronism."[17] At the same time the historian was deprived of his chair at the Collège by orders that originated with the Ministry of Education.[18] Incensed, the students of Paris immediately championed his cause. Already extremely popular, Michelet became overnight the symbol of political repression of academic freedom by an overbearing government. The silencing of Michelet was in the best tradition of the Mickiewicz and Quinet affairs. But the Michelet case, coming as it did at a time of political ferment, led to more serious agitation, proclamations, and demonstrations than had taken place in connection with Quinet. The culmination of a series of political banquets that provided a means to voice opposition to the government and a general dissatisfaction with the Guizot regime now combined with the dismissal of Michelet to create the antigovernment feeling the students poured out in the first weeks of 1848.

Yet another tempest arose in the months preceding the February Revolution, and, although it took place in the south of France, rumbles were to be felt in the principal student communities elsewhere in the country. In December, 1847, the popular dean of the medical school at Montpellier, Professor Berard, was relieved of his deanship and replaced by Professor Riber. This action was taken by the Ministry of Education because of Berard's outspoken criticism of the political regime of the monarchy. The medical students of Montpellier staged both peaceful and disruptive demonstrations in support of Berard and in opposition to the government.[19] From Lyon the medical students wrote condolences and praise to the former dean, while in Paris the students, already in a state of ferment over the Michelet affair, championed the cause of Professor Berard and renewed their denunciation of the Guizot government.[20]

The students' disaffection for the government had many facets. Along with the nation as a whole the students denounced the administration's foreign policy. Peace at any price may have been popular with French businessmen and in European courts, but it was not popular with the French populace. The students were in the front ranks of those nationalists who denounced as cowardly the government's timid handling of international affairs. They championed the cause of Polish independence and of Italian "liberation." "The holy cause of Poland," declared the student journal *La Lanterne du Quartier Latin* in its February, 1847, issue, "cannot be separated from that of France. This can never be forgotten by the democratic youth."[21] That this was no idle statement may be seen in the fact that more than twelve hundred students attended a manifestation organized by the schools of Paris to commemorate the anniversary of the insurrection of Krakow on February 22, 1847.[22] Italian liberation from Austrian domination was also a popular cause among French students,[23] and there was general sympathy with the oppressed Irish. In June, 1847, a *souscription* was taken up by the law students in Paris to aid the suffering Irish.[24]

These sentiments, which stemmed from student liberalism, led quite naturally to anti-Austrian, -Prussian, and -Russian feelings; and to a somewhat lesser extent to criticism of England. The students showed more tolerance toward England because of that country's parliamentary system of government based upon reforms of the 1830s. But as for the three autocratic regimes in central and eastern Europe, the students had only bitter criticism.[25] They resented the French government's cordial and cooperative diplomatic relations with these "oppressive" monarchies, and even chided Guizot, the minister of foreign affairs, for attending a party given by the Austrian ambassador.[26] Czar Nicholas I, who, incidentally, considered Louis Philippe a usurper because he had come to the throne of France by revolution, was referred to as *bête fauve* in *La Lanterne*.[27]

The students were also to the left of the ruling bourgeoisie on domestic affairs. The "average" Parisian student, who remains as ill-defined as the contemporary "silent majority," was not a political radical. However, he did hope to see changes in the political structure of the monarchy. In the years prior to 1848 he tended to be a curious mixture of idealism and pragmatism. Thus he rallied about the slogan of the Great Revolution: "Liberty, Equality, and Fraternity." When a number of political banquets were held during the summer and fall of 1847, the students expressed their approval of the banquets and of the reforms thereby implied.

The banquet campaign began as the work of those who constituted the moderate opposition to the government. There was nothing revolutionary about the reforms they advocated. They did not call for drastic change. The banqueteers were nearly all men of some means. They had no desire to change the prevailing social or economic structure, which assured for them security, comfort, and dominance. Nevertheless, the banquet campaign gave every Frenchman an opportunity to support, not necessarily by active participation, a faction in opposition to the government of Guizot and Louis Philippe. The general theme of the campaign was the support of the extension of the franchise to the middle class and of freedom of assembly. Other reforms were championed at particular banquets, but these two were basic.[28] The first of the banquets was held near Paris at Château-Rouge on July 9, 1847. It was heralded on the front page of *La Lanterne,* which declared the students to be in complete sympathy with its aims.[29]

Throughout France the students took an interest in the rash of banquets that followed the one at Château-Rouge, and in some instances they were even invited to take part. At a reform banquet held at Strasbourg in September and attended by five hundred and fifty, M. Keyser, a medical student at the University of Strasbourg, offered the following toast: "To youth's participation in electoral and parliamentary reform!"[30] At Dijon a banquet was held by more radical members of the Left on September 21. With Etienne Arago, Louis Blanc, and -Alexandre-Auguste Ledru-Rollin present, M. Quillot, a law student, offered a toast in the name of the schools of Paris. In it he declared that the students of Paris were happy to learn that the democratic principles were the foundation for the gathering, and hailed the great revolutionary concept "Liberty, Equality, and Fraternity."[31]

With the coming of winter the banquets (many of which were held out of doors) tapered off. Then in December two banquets were proposed to be held in the city of Paris, where hitherto none had taken place. One was to be organized by reformers of the Twelfth Arrondissement, many of them members of the National Guard, the other by the students of the schools of Paris. The students wanted to hold their own banquet in order to honor Michelet, Quinet, and other popular professors and to express their support for the independence these men had shown in the past.[32] However, the police, who followed very closely the activities of the students, repeatedly discovered the proposed location of the banquet and forced the proprietor to deny its use for what the government considered a dangerous and inflammatory gathering.[33] Thus the students were prevented from holding their banquet in December or January. When it became known that the Twelfth Arrondissement of Paris, which included the Latin Quarter, was to hold a banquet, the students abandoned their own plans and gave it their full support.

The preparations for the banquet of the Twelfth Arrondissement were originally dominated by the republican Left of the reform movement in the capital. Many were officers in the National Guard who themselves did not have the right to vote and who were generally dissatisfied with the government's unwillingness to embark upon a program that would include electoral reform. In order to give the banquet greater prestige, the more conservative deputies in the opposition faction in the chamber were invited to take part and to share in the planning. Although at first these deputies were reluctant to associate themselves with the radicals of the Twelfth Arrondissement, they either felt obligated to continue to support the banquet campaign or believed that through their participation they could inject a moderate and stabilizing influence into what they feared might turn into an explosive situation that would discredit the entire movement and nullify all that had been accomplished through the summer and fall. Thus it happened that the moderates not only took part in but also gained control of the arrangements for the banquet. They then moved it from a proposed location on the Left Bank in the Twelfth Arrondissement to one on the Right Bank, increased the entrance fee, and changed the date from a Sunday to a weekday. These changes were designed to lessen the influence of artisans and the working class and to make the affair more moderate and bourgeois.

Against this background the news of the cancellation of

Michelet's course broke over the Latin Quarter in the
first week of January. Already frustrated in their attempts to hold their own banquet, the students viewed
this new move on the part of the government as an
outrage, as further proof that the government was bent
on destroying the last remnants of academic freedom.
On January 4 a delegation of students presented the
newspapers of Paris with a statement expressing their
discontent. The following day it was printed by nine of
the city's journals: *La Réforme, Le National, La Démocratie
Pacifique, Le Siècle, La Patrie, Le Courrier Français, La
Gazette de France, L'Union Monarchique,* and *Le Commerce.*
The statement declared, in part:

> Youth in general, and the students in particular, protest ener-
> getically against this new arbitrary action on the part of the
> government. . . . We had three illustrious professors, Mickie-
> wicz, Quinet, and Michelet, men of genius and courage, and
> now—all three have been taken from us one after the other
> under different pretexts. But the true motive for their sup-
> pression is that their inspired words, burning and filled with
> truth, awakened in us sentiments of love of country, liberty
> and humanity. . . . Youth understands only too well the duties
> that the future imposes upon it, to raise a flag other than that
> of its immortal forebear. Youth will have many tormentors,
> who will forbid its reunions, try to disunite it, suspend the pro-
> fessors whom it loves and esteems, [but] it will never be dis-
> couraged. On the contrary, youth will redouble its unity, its
> strength, its energy and its courage, to resist those who op-
> press it: for the time of liberty approaches, and woe to those
> who try to crush it.[34]

On the morning of January 6 the students took their
cause into the streets. They gathered in the Place du
Panthéon, some two thousand in number, and made
their way in perfect order through the narrow streets of
the Latin Quarter. They arrived before the hotel
Flavacourt in the rue des Postes at noon—the hour at
which the suspended professor would have been giving
his lecture. Their purpose was to read to Michelet an
address of support and condolence; but, finding that he
was not at home, they left the address there for him to

read. "The students of the schools were truly indignant," it began, "as the result of the brutal inequitable measures that have struck your teaching!" They had come to protest once again the arbitrary use of power, the address continued, and the miserable shackles it had placed upon freedom of thought. This power issued from the barricades of 1830 and brought back to mind the worst days of the Bourbon Restoration. "To the Deputies, the electorate and the people, the challenge has already been made," it went on to say. "It is now the turn of the students who have been provoked by your dismissal. After Quinet, after Mickiewicz, after Berard, your independent voice has been stifled. You are guilty, sir, of speaking of progress and unity, guilty of exalting the glory of France and of dreaming of her grandeur and regeneration." The address concluded, "In losing you, sir, be convinced that our sympathy can only be increased and that we will always carry in our hearts the names of those who fought for liberty, truth and the rights of all."[35]

The students then moved off to the Institut de France in hope of finding Michelet there. Disappointed once again, they brought the learned members of that hallowed institution to the windows with shouts of "Down with Guizot! Down with Salvandy!" and "Long Live Michelet! Long live Quinet!" After the demonstration before the Institut, some of the students dispersed, going off to class or returning home. But most of them, more than fifteen hundred, decided to cross the Seine in order to thank the newspapers that were supporting them in this struggle for academic freedom. Maintaining perfect order the students proceeded to the offices of *Le National, La Réforme, Le Courrier Français* and the *La Démocratie Pacifique.* At each they sent in a delegation to express their gratitude, and the editors, in turn, confirmed their support of the students. It was late in the afternoon when they left the rue de Beaune, where the office of *La Démocratie Pacifique* was located, and made their way back to the Latin Quarter. There had been no violent or unruly behavior on the part of the students in this expression of their displeasure with the government's attitude and ac-

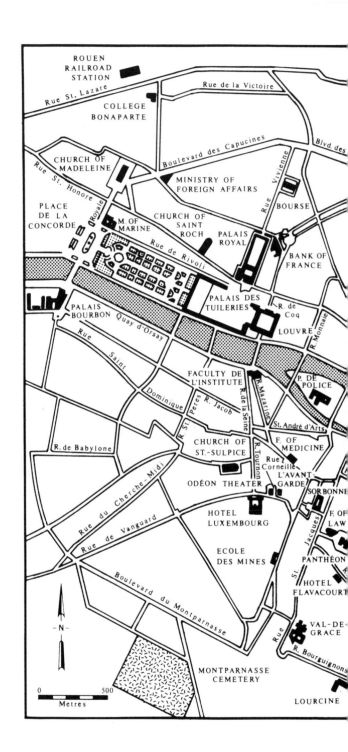

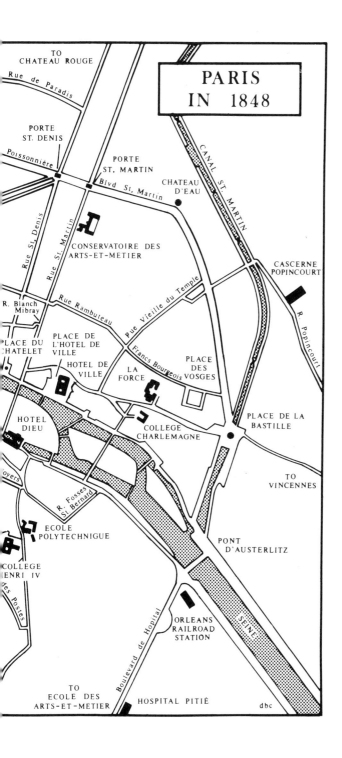

PARIS IN 1848

tions.[36] Since the dismissal of Quinet, Michelet had been the visible sign of antigovernment feelings in the schools of Paris. Now he became the martyr of that cause who would be avenged in the February Days.

The smoldering antagonism of the students in Paris came to the surface again early in February. This time a demonstration was organized jointly by the two student journals: *La Lanterne du Quartier-Latin* and *L'Avant-Garde*. The first of these journals to be established was *La Lanterne*. Located in the rue Saint-Jacques by February, 1848, it had published its first edition in January, 1847, with Antonio Watripon as chief editor. Watripon was twenty-five years of age and did not have the formal status of a student.[37] He was a capable journalist who had come to Paris from his home town of Beauvais and who had worked on the staff of *La Réforme*. Another of the editors of *La Lanterne* was Arthur Mangin, a law student. Priced at thirty-five centimes, the eight-page *La Lanterne* was published monthly, usually appearing during the third week. In politics it was both democratic and republican, with occasional undertones of utopian socialism. All articles in the journal were directed at the student population of Paris—and of France. They contained news of the schools of Paris and of the provinces, lectures by Watripon on the duties of students, reprints of Michelet's lectures, theatrical news, and so on.

L'Avant-Garde, which bore the subtitle *Journal des Ecoles*, was founded in January, 1848, following a split in the ranks of the supporters of *La Lanterne*.[38] Only two issues appeared before the February Revolution but, like *La Lanterne*, it was an immediate success with the students. Also like its counterpart—with which good relations were maintained despite some basic differences of opinion—it was directed at the student population of Paris.[39] However, *L'Avant-Garde* started out to be more literary and more wordy; it contained more than four times the pages of *La Lanterne*. Its chief editor, Henri Antoine Bosselet, was a young Parisian of thirty years of age who lived with his father, a member of the Bureau de bienfaisance ("relief committee"). By the middle of February, 1848, both journals had come under the surveillance of the Paris police. In a letter from the prefect of police, M. Gabriel Delessert, to the minister of justice both journals were described as "anarchistic" and "subversive," and their editors were singled out as troublemakers.[40]

The February 3 demonstration was the well-organized work of the staffs of the two papers. The purpose of the demonstration was to present to the Chamber of Deputies a petition, signed by the students, demanding freedom of thought for the faculties of Paris that had been violated in the cases of Mickiewicz, Quinet, and Michelet. The students began to gather after lunch in the Place du Panthéon, the traditional place of assembly for their manifestations. By 1:30 P.M. they numbered more than three thousand. With Bosselet, Watripon, Mangin, and M. Joubert (an editor of *La Lanterne*) at their head, the students marched three by three in good order and in silence toward the Palais-Bourbon, which housed the Chamber of Deputies. The column wound its way through the streets of the Left Bank: down the rue de la Sorbonne to the rue de la Harpe, through the Place de l'Ecole de Médecine, down the rue de la Seine to the quais, and along the river to the Place du Palais-Bourbon.

The students were met at the entrance to the Place by a small number of police. In accordance with their prearranged plans to stay within the law, they sent a delegation of five to enter the Palais-Bourbon while the rest waited calmly along the quai. The student delegation, led by L. Polge, a recent law school graduate,[41] was ushered into the *salle des pas perdus* ("waiting room") where it was received by Adolphe Crémieux, a liberal member of the Chamber of Deputies. He took the petition and assured the students that he would make it known to the Chamber. The deputy then agreed to go out to the quai and address the students. As the delegation, accompanied by Crémieux, approached the students, one of the five shouted "Voici Monsieur Crémieux!" His comrades enthusiastically shouted their unanimous approval, and breaking their ranks that they had maintained since assembling before the Panthéon, swarmed about the deputy. Violence at this point was only narrowly avoided. While the student delegation had been inside the Palais-Bourbon, mounted troops, of both regular cavalry and the Municipal Guard, had converged upon the Place du Palais-Bourbon and were poised in readiness to disperse the marchers. Seeing the potential danger, Crémieux addressed the students: "Gentlemen, your demonstration has been to this point beautiful, magnificent; you have remained within the limits of the law; but now you can go no further without violating the law. The members of the commission have given me your petition; it will be deposited by me in the bureau of the Chamber. Return, gentlemen, in the same good order to the Latin Quarter from which you have come."[42] Upon hearing these words the students again formed their column and withdrew along the quai.

They did not, however, go back to the Latin Quarter. Instead, they crossed the Seine by the Pont Royal, passed by the Tuileries, and arrived before the offices of *Le National*. A member of the delegation that had entered the Palais-Bourbon, M. Levasseur, entered the building and read to the editors the petition that had been presented to the Chamber of Deputies. This statement, read by M. Crémieux to the Chamber and published in the opposition press, was as follows:

Mr. President, and Deputies: We the undersigned, students of the schools of Paris and auditors of the Collège de France, have the honor of declaring to you the following:

The chairs of Mickiewicz, Quinet, and Michelet having been successively taken away by the Minister of Public Instruction who acted in violation of the law. . . .

The suspension of these chairs, or merely the suspension of these professors is a grave blow to higher education, to its independence, and thus to the freedom of thought guaranteed by the Charter.

We come to ask you, gentlemen, to oppose the arbitrary

actions of the ministerial authority toward the law and to have
our professors, whose words we cherish, returned to us, because these words inspire us and raise our spirits.

We have the honor of being,

Your very humble and obedient servants.[43]

The students then heard kind words from the editor
and moved on to the offices of *La Réforme, Le Courrier
Français,* and *La Démocratie Pacifique,* where the same
ceremony was repeated. Then, satisfied that their declaration would be heard by the government and made
known to the nation as a whole, they returned to the Place
du Panthéon and disbanded.

The manifestation had once again been peaceful and
the students had violated no laws. But their words had
grown sharper and their numbers larger. The young
people who marched on February 3 were representative
of the student population of Paris; they were not, as the
Journal des débats a semiofficial government publication,
alleged, the troublemakers of the Left Bank who demon-
strated just for the pleasure of raising hell.[44]

In the wake of the demonstrations that followed the
suspension of Michelet, the government launched an
investigation of student activities in Paris. Files were
compiled on the two student journals and a relatively new
student association was uncovered. The Commission de
secours des écoles had been founded in late 1846 by
students of the various schools in the capital. The purpose of the association, according to police reports, was to
serve as a pretext for political meetings that were illegal
without government permission. Its members were
young men, forty-nine in all, "most of whom were known
for their republican views and turbulent character."[45]
Above the association's bylaws the epigraph read "Liberty, Equality, Fraternity." Another document, which fell
into the hands of the police, conjured up shades of the
Abbé Sieyes's famous pamphlet on the Third Estate; it
read in part: "What are the people? — Nothing. What
ought they be? — Everything."[46] The association also had
the support of a number of university professors. When

the revolution broke out on February 22, the government was preparing to move against this "anarchist" organization, as it was referred to by the police.[47]

Plans for the banquet to be held in the Twelfth Arrondissement of Parish had become generally known during the early weeks of January, 1848. Three separate student committees had been formed in order to coordinate the diffused efforts of the numerous schools of Paris. The banquet committee had proposed to give the students fifty free tickets so that the schools would be represented. However, when the committee was reorganized on February 15 in such a manner as to place effective control in the hands of the more moderate, dynastic opposition, a split occurred in the ranks of the students. Two of the three student committees were willing to support the moderates' limited political goals—that is, the extension of the voting franchises and the right of peaceful assembly. But the third student committee, which was led by Antonio Watripon and which enjoyed the greatest influence and student support, rallied about Ledru-Rollin and the radical opposition.[48]

With the reorganization of the committee and the relocation of the site, the banquet no longer represented the Twelfth Arrondissement. But, despite the fact that it had lost most of its radical, that is, republican, characteristics, the government remained uneasy. A substantial number of the students, those adhering to the Watripon committee, withdrew their support. Even before February 15 the students had demanded that fifty free tickets, the same number as were to have been given to them, be given to workers so that the working class would be represented. The refusal on the part of the organizing committee had displeased the more democratic students and had led them to threaten that they would not attend unless the workers were represented.[49]

The cordial relationship that existed between the university students and the workers of Paris dated back to the revolution of 1830, when a relatively small number of students[50] and the workers had fought side by side on the barricades to overthrow the Bourbon monarchy. The students had, in varying degrees, continued to support the Parisian workers in demonstrations, and even in "rebellion" (1834), during the July Monarchy. On July 14, 1847, the students had sponsored a joint banquet with the workers in Paris to celebrate the Great Revolution.

The banquet itself was of a modest nature, but the toasts that followed were significant. They began with a young man from the business community who offered toasts "To the France of 1789 that attacked the Bastille!" and "To the France of 1830 that had defended liberty!" He was followed by a worker whose toast was "To the indissolvable fraternity of the sons of the proletariat and the bourgeoisie!" Then a student rose and offered a toast "To the union of the Schools and the People based upon the sacred principle of equality!"[51] All then stood and sang the *Marseillaise* before departing. This public display of friendship and unity between the proletariat and the sons of the bourgeoisie was quite unusual. "In 1830, and no doubt even earlier," wrote *La Lanterne* following the banquet, "our elder brothers of the schools had fraternized with the people in combat; but, strange as it may seem, these same men who were truly brothers of the proletariat in battle, in all probability would not have dined in public with one of them three months later; and on their part the proletarian would have refused such an invitation."[52] The "liberty" of which the young businessman spoke and the "sacred principle of equality" invoked by the student would bind them to the workers in February, 1848, when they would, together, overthrow the monarchy. However, when the artisans and workers returned to the barricades in June, liberty and equality took on quite different meanings for student and worker.

As the date for the banquet approached, the government became uneasy. Then, on the eve of the proposed festivity, the opposition newspapers published an account of what was to take place on February 22. The protest banquet was presented in such a manner as to cause the government great concern. The banqueteers were to assemble before the Madeleine and then march to Chaillot district, where the banquet would take place, escorted by unarmed members of the National Guard and by students. The council of ministers met on the morning of the twenty-first and assumed the position that the banqueteers were, in effect, calling out the National Guard. Such a call was a violation of the law of March 22, 1831, and could be interpreted as an act of rebellion. The council thereupon instructed the prefect of police to forbid the banquet and to invite the population to remain calm.

The principal deputies of the opposition, who planned to attend the banquet, were notified of the ban. They met that night at the home of Odilon Barrot to determine their course of action. They believed that they had the right to assemble peacefully; but they also conceded that the government had the right to forbid such a demonstration and meeting. In the end they voted eighty to seventeen not to attend the banquet. Although Alphonse de Lamartine and Edmond, count of Alton-Shée voted with the minority, they accepted the decision of their comrades. The news of the deputies' "defection," as it was viewed by the Left, led the organizing committee to call off the banquet.

The student groups that had supported the banquet, despite its moderate drift, were disappointed and frustrated. Unable to hold a banquet of their own, they were now deprived of taking part in this political manifestation against the government. Furthermore, the Watripon committee had planned to hold a student banquet following that of the Twelfth Arrondissement. Very little is known about this proposed banquet. On the last page of the February, 1848, issue of *L'Avant-Garde* there appears a simple statement: "The Banquet of the Schools will follow immediately that of the Twelfth Arrondissement."

The stage was thus set for the events of February 22–24. Yet, if the government was caught by surprise, it was not the fault of the police. Delessert had carried out his duties as prefect: he knew what was going on in Paris and he informed the government.[53] He had spies everywhere, who had infiltrated the secret societies of the workers, reported on the activities of the students, and kept their fingers on the very pulse of the city. On February 15 he alerted the government in a letter: "There exists in Paris a restlessness caused by apprehensions that the banquet will be accompanied by trouble; certainly the population is quite calm. . . . There is little activity in the business community."[54]

It is difficult to blame either the king or his government for not preparing for a revolution. The July Monarchy had weathered numerous crises that beforehand had appeared more explosive than did the approaching banquet. The limited military preparations and the cancellation of the banquet seemed adequate measures to men who were not novices in such matters.

.II.

The Making of a Rebellion:
February 22 and 23

February 22

On the morning of February 22, Parisians began to gather in the square before the church of the Madeleine. This traditional meeting place for the opposition had been designated as the rallying point for those who were to take part in the banquet. Despite the light rain that fell that Tuesday morning, a considerable number had arrived in the square by nine o'clock. Some of them had not received the news that the banquet had been canceled, whereas others had come out of curiosity to see what might happen. The crowd was leaderless and in a holiday mood. It was made up of a cross section of the population ranging from workers and artisans to well-dressed bourgeois men and women. Calm prevailed as the morning wore on.[1]

Across the Seine in the heart of the Latin Quarter, another gathering, potentially more explosive, was taking place. In the Place du Panthéon a mixture of students and other young persons had assembled for the purpose of marching to the Madeleine in protest of the cancellation of the banquet. The students believed that they had been betrayed by the deputies of the opposition and deserted by the organizers of the banquet.[2] The Watripon committee, which had opposed the February 15 reorganization of the banquet committee and the banquet's relocation from the Left Bank, was the motivating force for this demonstration. Its members had held a

32

meeting sometime after midnight of the twenty-first after hearing of the cancellation of the banquet and had decided to defy the government by holding a demonstration on the twenty-second.[3] More than three hundred young men were assembled by 10:00 A.M. in the Place du Panthéon. Although most were students such as Charles Bellan and Edouard M. Commelin,[4] some, according to *Le Moniteur,* were "those individuals with sinister faces, who are found on every occasion of trouble with the schools."[5] These "sinister faces" belonged not to the students but to ardent revolutionaries such as Wilfried de Fonvielle, a professor of mathematics, and to workers such as Adolphe Chenu. *La Lanterne* also states that there were "men from the Faubourg Saint-Marceau."[6] Claude L. Giubega, a law student who took part in the demonstration, referred to the group as a "student corps,"[7] but the evidence available indicates that the "leaders," to the extent that there was leadership, were not students. Watripon was perhaps the principal figure at the Panthéon. Bosselet, editor of *L'Avant-Garde,* was also there. As the day progressed others emerged at the head of the demonstration: Wilfried de Fonvielle; a young Belgium printer, M. Debock; a young engraver, M. Jourdain; and a young journalist, Philippe Faure.[8]

Philippe Faure, who kept a diary of events before and during the February Days, was so sure that there would be fighting on the twenty-second that he sat down at 5 o'clock that morning to make out his last will and testament. "I am going to fight for Liberty, not for a party," he wrote during the early hours of that historic day. "It is a duty for me, a journalist, to take up arms," he continued, and concluded by asking God's pardon: "Pardon us, divine Jesus, if we do not know how to prefer martyrdom to combat, as you did!"[9]

At ten o'clock the demonstrators formed themselves into ranks of three and prepared to march through the streets of the Left Bank, cross the river, and go on to the Madeleine, where they planned to arrive at eleven, the original time for the rally of the banqueteers. They descended the rue Saint-Jacques singing the *Marseillaise.*

Then veering left they marched to the Place de l'Ecole de Médecine where they were joined by medical students and young men from the district. Their number increased as they made their way to the Carrefour de Bussi (Buci), down the rue Dauphine, and across the Pont Neuf. On the Right Bank the students and young men of the Latin Quarter were joined by artisans who closed their shops and by workers who left their jobs. Gaining the rue Saint-Honoré by way of the rue de la Monnaie, the marchers arrived in the Place de la Madeleine singing the more revolutionary *Chant des Girondins,* which was currently very popular in Paris:[10]

> Par sa voix le canon appelle
> De la France tous les enfants,
> Et pour vaincre ou mourir pour elle
> Voyez venir ces combattants.
> Mourir pour la patrie, mourir pour la patrie,
> C'est le sort le plus beau, le plus
> digne d'envie. . . .[11]

Their number had more than doubled since leaving the Panthéon. The march had been orderly and without incident.

Upon reaching the square before the neoclassical, temple-like church, the students and workers found a crowd of about fifteen hundred persons milling about aimlessly. The newcomers gave it direction. Now several thousand strong, the people were led down the rue Royale and into the Place de la Concorde. Since there was to be no banquet, they would go instead to the Chamber of Deputies at the Palais Bourbon and there protest the violation of their freedom to assemble peacefully.

As the multitudes milled about the enormous Place de la Concorde, once named "Place de la Révolution," a small group, which included Faure, Jourdain, Debock, Fonvielle, and Commelin, approached the Pont de la Concorde. The bridge over the Seine, which led to the Palais-Bourbon, was guarded by seventeen municipal guardsmen on foot. M. Lemoine-Tascherat, one of the two police commissioners charged with maintaining

order in and about the Place de la Concorde, had quickly
formed these troops. As the group of young men approached the bridge, the guardsmen fixed their bayonets
and cocked their muskets. With bayonets at their chests,
relates Faure, the young men hailed the troops: "Comrades, you would not shoot your brothers? We are peaceful, as you can see; but if you fire on us you are lost
because you are only a few. Therefore let us pass."[12]
While still speaking, first Fonvielle and then several
others passed through the weak line to a point behind the
guardsmen. There followed a brief scuffle in which no
one was harmed, but Faure had cocked the pistol he was
carrying. The guardsmen, hopelessly outnumbered,
gave way as the crowd surged forward across the
bridge.[13]

A second version of the incident was given by
Lemoine-Tascherat. When the demonstrators moved
down the rue Royale into the Place de la Concorde, the
two police commissioners found themselves with only a
handful of men, a totally inadequate force to control
several thousand invaders. Therefore, Lemoine-
Tascherat rushed to the Pont de la Concorde to prevent
the mob from crossing the Seine to reach the Chamber of
Deputies while his colleague, M. Martinet, went to the
Préfecture de Police to obtain help. The mob was in a
nasty mood, recorded Lemoine-Tascherat, and became
very irritated at the obstacle he presented on the bridge.
"Into the river with the commissioner!" they shouted,
"Into the river with the Muncipal Guard!" Lemoine-
Tascherat continued his account: "We were overpow-
ered. I ordered the men to return to their quarters. I was
struck from behind, on the shoulder, by a student! . . .
The column [which crossed the bridge] was made up of a
large number of workers and some students; there were
also several national guardsmen with their sabers, these
alone were armed."[14] On this latter point Lemoine-
Tascherat was certainly wrong. Although he had no way
of knowing, Faure, by his own admission, carried a pistol.
It would seem quite likely that others in the circle in
which Faure moved also were armed, but there is no

indication that any of the students had come prepared for serious fighting.

Passing over the Seine the crowd advanced upon the Palais-Bourbon. Then with shouts of "Down with Guizot!" and "Long live Reform!" they scaled the high iron fence that surrounded the building. As the Chamber of Deputies was not yet in session for the day, there was no one to receive them. They milled about the square before the building and its grounds, but made only feeble—and unsuccessful—attempts to enter the palace. Shortly after noon General Tiburce Sebastiani, commander of the Garrison of Paris, arrived on the scene and called for troops to restore order. A squadron of cavalry, supported by a battalion of the line and with five more battalions in reserve, advanced along the quai d'Orsay and drove the people back across the river into the Place de la Concorde. Although the soldiers inflicted very little violence, the crowd became angry and began to stone the troops. Sebastiani then gave orders to clear the Place de la Concorde. This time, however, it was the hated Municipal Guard, wielding sabers with deadly effect, that charged into the crowd. The bloodhsed that began in the Place de la Concorde was to continue for three days.[15]

The first student to spill his blood in the February Days was Charles L. Giubega. The twenty-one-year-old law student had marched from the Panthéon with the students in the morning, but, when the others crossed the river to the Palais-Bourbon, he had gone with a band of demonstrators to the Ministry of Foreign Affairs. At the Ministry they shouted "Long live Reform!" and "Down with Guizot!" Then a troop of mounted municipal guardsmen arrived and charged into the crowd in order to drive it from the square before the Ministry. The people picked up stones and threw them at the troops. Giubega, after hurling his last stone, was ridden down by one of the horsemen. He was helped to his feet by a worker and taken to a nearby bookstore, where his wounds were washed. His left arm and leg were injured. Taken to his room at 14, rue de l'Ecole de Médecine, he was attended by a physician. Giubega remained in bed until the afternoon of the twenty-fourth, when he limped out to see firsthand the progress of the revolution.[16]

Most of the students returned to the Latin Quarter and proceeded to disrupt the tranquility that had prevailed during the afternoon. At the same time groups of varying sizes, determined to vent their anger on whatever form of authority they might happen to encounter, fanned out on the Right Bank. Two of the larger bands of demonstrators, each numbering in the hundreds, harassed troops in the Place de la Madeleine and before the Ministry of Foreign Affairs. They stoned the soldiers and shouted "Down with Guizot!" and "Long live Reform!" A third column marched through the streets to the Bourse and on to the Place de la Bastille. They not only shouted their displeasure with the government, but also actually broke into an arms shop on the rue Neuve-Vivienne. Late in the afternoon barricades began to appear between the Place de la Madeleine and the Place du Palais-Royal. Although these demonstrators were primarily workers, artisans, and of the lower bourgeoisie the students were also active.

It is reported that the first stone for the barricade built across the rue de Rivoli before the Ministry of the Marine was pried up by the cane of a law student, M. Presseq.[17] Edouard M. Commelin, twenty-three, who had marched from the Panthéon in the morning, helped to build barricades in the rue de Rivoli and, after being driven from them, worked on the barricade in the rue Saint-Honoré before the church of Saint-Roch.[18] Charles Bellan, a twenty-five-year-old law student whose trousers had been pierced by a bayonnet in the scuffle on the Pont de la Concorde in the morning, also worked on the first barricade in the rue Saint-Honoré at the rue du Coq. Bellan, who was unarmed on the twenty-second, was forced to abandon the structure about 10:00 P.M. when it was attacked by army units.[19] A medical student, Auguste Corlieu, twenty-two, was also active on this first day of fighting. Although there is no evidence that Corlieu took part in the fighting, he did aid the wounded in the rue Saint-Martin.[20]

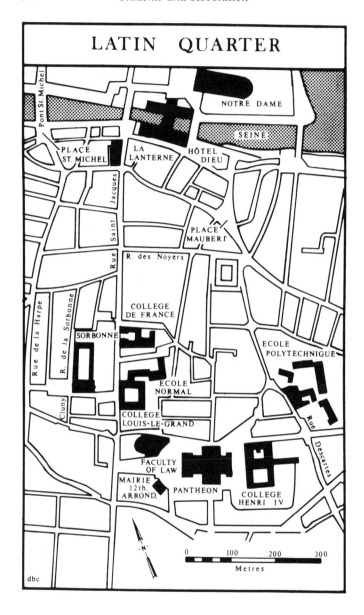

LATIN QUARTER

Pont St. Michel

NOTRE DAME

SEINE

PLACE
ST. MICHEL

LA
LANTERNE

HÔTEL
DIEU

Rue Saint Jacques

PLACE
MAUBERT

R. des Noyers

Rue de la Harpe

R. de la Sorbonne

COLLEGE
DE FRANCE

SORBONNE

ECOLE
POLYTECHNIQUE

Cluny

ECOLE
NORMAL

COLLEGE
LOUIS-LE-GRAND

Rue Descartes

FACULTY
OF LAW

MAIRIE
12th.
ARROND.

PANTHEON

COLLEGE
HENRI IV

N

0   100   200   300
Metres

dbc

Watripon, who took part in the work on the barricade in the rue Saint-Honoré wrote the following of the affair:

"It was evident to us [referring to the bloodshed in the Place de la Concorde] that the fighting had begun; . . . we also thought that it was necessary for us to stay near the streets as the commotion gained step by step with equal possibility in one quarter or another. . . . It took us twenty minutes for this operation [the building of the barricade before the Ministry of the Marine]. Around us the workers in their blouses became impatient to see it take us so long. They therefore quickly went in groups of six or seven to the huge iron fence under the arcades of the Ministry. The fencing was twisted as if by magic; with the aid of the bars that were used as levers, the paving stones were easily pried up. They tried to overturn several carriages to make barricades, but the crowd was not of one mind on that task. It was then that the mounted Municipal Guard, which had approached the street, charged us. They pursued us along the rue de Rivoli under the arcades. The confusion was horrible, men, women, and children found themselves caught up in the confusion and crushed under foot. A young woman fell wounded on my left; a saber blow fell on another young man at the same time and he lost his vision.
The people withdrew to the rue Saint-Honoré, where they began to build more barricades. It was there that we can say the fighting really began.[21]

These hastily erected barricades were poorly defended for the most part by unarmed men. By 6 P.M. the government's forces had driven the people from them and there was no organized opposition. The night was relatively calm on the Right Bank, although several arms shops were broken into by the people and pillaged.[22]
On the Left Bank there were also demonstrations. The students returning from the Palais-Bourbon and the Place de la Concorde marched noisily through the Latin Quarter. One band of students accompanied by young workers went to the Ecole Polytechnique in order to encourage its students to join the antigovernment demonstrations. The students and workers on the Left Bank looked to the *polytechniciens,* with their military training and arms, for leadership. They deemed it extremely

important that these 240[23] young men joined the rebellion and give it some sort of direction and prestige.

The students of the Ecole Polytechnique enjoyed a certain reputation, which far surpassed justification, because of their role in the revolution of 1830. The school had been founded by the revolutionary government in 1794 to help fill the vacuum created by the new emphasis on the sciences and by the closing of the church-affiliated schools. The *polytechniciens* seem always to been one revolution behind the government. When Napoleon visited the school in the early days of the Empire, he is reported to have said to the director, Gaspard Monge, "Your students do not like me." To which Monge replied, "Sire, it was only with great difficulty that we made republicans of them, you must give them time to become imperialists. You have formed too quick a judgment."[24] By March, 1814, the *polytechniciens* were defending the city of Paris for Napoleon against the attacking Allied armies. In 1816 the school was closed and the students were sent home because of their Bonapartist sentiments. When the revolution of 1830 broke out Charles X closed the schools at once (July 27) because of the overt antigovernment sentiments of the students. Most of the *polytechniciens* went home but about sixty of them joined the revolution. One of the students, M. Vaneau, was killed when he was struck in the head by a musket ball, and others, MM. Baduel, Lothon, and d'Ouvrier, were wounded.[25] However, the students were not long satisfied with the new bourgeois regime.

Republican sentiments were openly expressed in 1832 when the students shouted "Vive Lafayette! Vive la République!" at a banquet given in honor of the "hero of two worlds."[26] Before the year was out the government had closed the school and sent the students home. Again, in December, 1834, half of the student body was expelled for two weeks. In 1844 the government found it necessary to close the school once more. This last closing of the school before 1848 was not so much the result of political agitation as it was a national manifestation in support of government policy.[27] Thus their history of conflict with the government-appointed school administration and with the government itself had gained for the students of the Ecole Polytechnique a reputation of independence, action, and defiance.

On the eve of the revolution of 1848 the *polytechniciens* were once again engaged in a conflict with the established order. This time politics had little to do with the affair. Rather, it stemmed from the students' hatred of Paul-François Dubois, professor of literature at the school. Dubois, because of his numerous other activities—he was a member of the Chamber of Deputies and a director of the Ecole Normale, among other things—did not prepare for his classes. His students all signed a letter asking for his dismissal. When the professor refused to resign and the administration did nothing, they disrupted the class until it was necessary for the school authorities to step in and to punish the students.[28]

The Dubois affair completely absorbed the energies and attention of the *polytechniciens* in the days prior to February 22. Furthermore, it should be pointed out that these students had shown little interest in the banquet campaign, nor had they taken part in the pro-Michelet manifestations of January and early February. They were not at all prepared psychologically for the coming political revolution.

The students of the Ecole Polytechnique, within the confines of its walls, knew nothing of the events of the morning and afternoon of Februry 22. At about 7 P.M., while they were sitting in a study hall, they heard first the drums calling out the National Guard of the Twelfth Arrondissement and then the students and workers singing the *Marseillaise* and the *Chant des Girondins* and shouting "Vive l'Ecole Polytechnique!" Voices called upon the students to come out and join the "people" as they had in earlier years. Newspapers and proclamations were thrown over the walls to inform the isolated *polytechniciens* of what was taking place in the city. But before the demonstrators could gain entrance and before the students inside became aware of what was really happening, the Municipal Guard arrived and drove the crowd off.[29] The

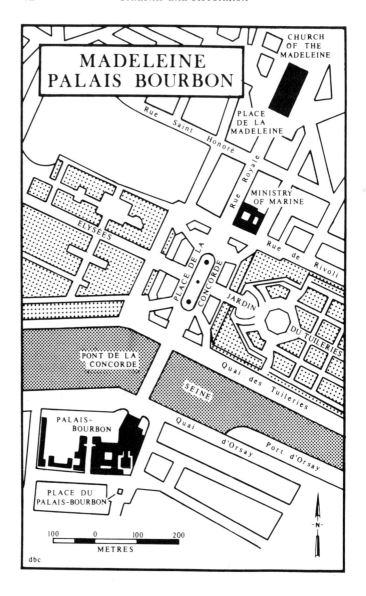

CHURCH OF THE MADELEINE

MADELEINE
PALAIS BOURBON

Rue Saint Honoré

PLACE DE LA MADELEINE

Rue Royale

MINISTRY OF MARINE

ELYSÉES

Rue de Rivoli

PLACE DE LA

CONCORDE

JARDIN

DU TUILERIES

PONT DE LA CONCORDE

Quai des Tuileries

SEINE

PALAIS-BOURBON

Quai d'Orsay

Port d'Orsay

PLACE DU PALAIS-BOURBON

-N-

100   0   100   200
METRES

dbc

Latin Quarter was relatively quiet during the remainder of the night although small groups of students and workers were to be seen about the streets in the hours before midnight.[30]

The students from the *collèges* of Paris had taken no part in the events of February 22, but the late afternoon and evening was disrupted for them by the return of the students from the Palais-Bourbon. Henri Dabot wrote to his parents from the collège Louis-le-Grand in the heart of the Latin Quarter: "We heard continually shouts urging the students on. . . . There was no studying at all done during this period. . . . They returned later and we heard them yelling near the Collège de France. They had gone to the Ecole Polytechnique to get the students there to join them."[31]

On the night of the twenty-second the deputies of the opposition met at the residence of Odilon Barrot. They were in the process of drawing up a list of accusations against the Guizot government that they planned to present to the Chamber of Deputies when a self-appointed deputation of students arrived in the street before the house. The students demanded an account of the actions of the deputies and an explanation of their "defection." Several of the students were admitted, and Barrot, as spokesman for the opposition, explained to them the reasons that had led him and his colleagues to withdraw their support from the proposed banquet. As reported two days later in *Le Siècle,* Barrot "told them that the ministry wanted to substitute a bloody struggle [for a peaceful banquet] and in preparation it had assembled large numbers of troops, arms, and munitions. . . . It was important that order be maintained so that the ministry would not have a pretext to crush the voice of public opinion in blood. . . . The leader of the Left concluded by inviting the deputation to inform the students of the truth and to tell them not to engage in violent resistance."[32]

The events of February 22 were indecisive; but a major demonstration had taken place and blood had been shed. The students and other young men from the Left Bank had been the directing force in the demonstrations that had taken place. Their objectives had been limited to liberal reform and their method to nonviolent civil disobedience. The violence that occurred during the afternoon and evening of the twenty-second, minimal though it was, led to more serious conflicts and open hostility on the twenty-third.

February 23

On the morning of February 23 the government was still firmly entrenched and in control of the situation. There was, to be sure, cause for alarm, but no real indication of the events that were to take place in the next forty-eight hours. During the preceding night pockets of resistance had developed on the Right Bank. These centered primarily in the Saint-Denis and Saint-Martin districts of the city. Barricades had been built and were manned by armed workers and artisans. Fighting was sporadic and limited to these few sections of the city.

The key to the military—and thus the political— situation was the National Guard. The defense of the city of Paris and the stability of the July Monarchy depended upon the support of the National Guard. This armed militia was enrolled exclusively from the ranks of the bourgeoisie and was organized into thirteen legions, twelve corresponding to the twelve *arrondissements* of Paris and one legion of cavalry. If the National Guard had turned out in full strength and had energetically supported the government of Louis Philippe, perhaps even Guizot could have weathered the storm. But the members of the National Guard were not of one mind on February 23. The First, Tenth, and Eleventh legions and the mounted guardsmen were the most loyal during the February Days, whereas the Second, Fourth, Sixth, Seventh, and Ninth legions were hesitant. The three remaining legions, the Third, Eighth, and Twelfth, openly supported the antigovernment forces. Within each legion were, to be sure, men who differed from the majority, but the foregoing may be used as a good rule of thumb.

The Twelfth Legion, in particular, was hostile toward the government. Its officers had been among the original organizers of the canceled banquet and its rank and file were recruited from the middle and the lower bourgeoisie of one of the poorer *arrondissements* of Paris. Colonel G. Lavocat, commander of the Twelfth, gave the following account before the Cour d'Appel de Paris, which investigated the February Days:

> On the night of February 22, I ordered the call to arms. Very few men answered the call, fifty or sixty at most. They arrived at their meeting place, the Place du Panthéon, in a state of exasperation. They uttered cries of "Long live Reform! Down with Guizot! Down with Louis Philippe!" and they wanted to force me to do the same. They made menacing gestures toward me. I resisted them and realized the necessity to send them home in order to avoid a scandal; but, as they refused to obey that order, I ordered them to do patrol duty. They had been backed up by a considerable number of unarmed people, and other national guardsmen, unarmed but in uniform, who uttered the same cries.[33]

Lavocat, who had informed the minister of the interior on February 19 that his men were antigovernment and could not be counted on to act against the banqueteers,[34] was completely helpless and eventually dismissed his men.

On the morning of the twenty-third, when Lavocat again called out his guardsmen in accordance with orders he had received, they were in the same ugly mood as during the night before. Some two hundred strong in the Place du Panthéon, they shouted "Vive la République!" and gave more indications of supporting the defenders of the barricades than of suppressing them.

The principal difficulty on the twenty-third was the indecision of the government and of the troops upon whom it depended for its survival. Too many commanding officers sat idly in their headquarters without orders while the revolution gained momentum. Swift and deci-

sive action on the twenty-third, even without the support
of the unhappy National Guard units, might have kept
the situation under control.

The more radical student groups had spent the late
hours of the twenty-second in making plans for the next
day. The offices of *La Lanterne* and *L'Avant-Garde* served
as the headquarters for student activities. Rumors were
numerous and, in most cases, there was no way to con-
firm or refute them. The students made two major decisions early on the twenty-third. First, as there were no
centers of resistance on the Left Bank, they decided to
march in a body to the Right Bank and to take part in the
fighting that was reported already in progress at Saint-
Denis, at Saint-Martin, and in the Marais. They would
gather beforehand in the Place du Panthéon as they had
on the twenty-second. Second, a "reserve corps" of students would go to the Ecole Polytechnique and demand
that its students join the demonstrations. Rumor had it
that the *polytechniciens* were confined to their quarters
and that their swords and uniforms had been taken from
them.[35]

The rumor concerning the Ecole Polytechnique
proved to be unfounded. When the reserve corps arrived
before the school in force, the *polytechniciens*, in full uniform and with swords, marched out into the streets of
Paris in perfect formation. They had met earlier in their
large amphitheater amid great excitement. The commander of the school, General Jacques Aupick, appealed
to the students not to go out into the city even though it
was Wednesday and there were no classes. Aupick, who
had been at the school only a short time, was both respected and admired by the students. He was a graduate
of Saint-Cyr (1809) and as a young officer had served
under Napoleon at Leipzig. Nevertheless, the students
did not take the advice of their commander. In his presence a vote was taken and the *polytechniciens*, by a sizable
majority but not unanimously, declared that they would
go out into the city for the expressed purpose of putting
an end to the useless bloodshed. The method they proposed to employ was to place themselves between the

government's troops and the defenders of the barricades. Because of their immense popularity with the people of Paris and with the army as well, they believed that their action would stop the shooting on both sides. There is no indication that they had given any thought to what would happen once the fighting had stopped. The *polytechniciens* were not politically or socially motivated and do not appear to have had any real understanding of just what was taking place outside the walls of their school.[36]

Following the vote the students dressed in their best uniforms and, buckling on their swords, formed ranks in preparation to march. General Aupick, who was attached by personal ties to the Orleans family—he had been an *aide de camp* to the king's son, the Duke of Nemour— made no attempt to interfere with the students once their decision had been made. The big gates swung open into the rue Descartes about 10 A.M. and the *polytechniciens* marched out in parade formation. The crowd in the street roared its approval. They knew nothing of the decision made by the students to play a peacemaker's role in the developing struggle. The Parisians and the students from *L'Avant-Garde* were sure that the *polytechniciens* were coming out to take an active part in opposing the government. However, the students marched to the Place du Panthéon and presented themselves before the *mairie* of the Twelfth Arrondissement. The two student commanders explained the intentions of the *polytechniciens*, and, in consultation with the authorities present, it was decided to divide the students into twelve equal groups and to send them to the twelve *arrondissements* of Paris in order to stop the fighting. The student corps then separated itself into twelve formations. Each was composed of two classes: one first-year class and one second-year class. They then set out for the *mairies* of the assigned *arrondissements* accompanied by national guardsmen.[37]

As the *polytechniciens* marched through the streets of Paris, clearly identified by the uniforms they wore, they were greeted on all sides by cheers and shouts of support.

Believing they had come to take up the cause of the insurgents, the crowds cheered enthusiastically. The soldiers of the line and the National Guard opened their ranks respectfully and allowed the young men to pass. But, in fact, the *polytechniciens* took almost no part in the events of February 23. Shortly after they had departed from the Panthéon, news of the dismissal of Guizot spread rapidly through the city. Both sides broke off the fighting and it appeared, for several hours at least, that the rebellion would come to a "successful" conclusion. Thus the *polytechniciens* stood about in front of the *mairies* of the various *arrondissements* throughout the afternoon hours, and then returned to their school satisfied that all had gone well.

Not all the students of the Ecole Polytechnique were in agreement with the neutral role voted by the majority. Some of the more radical strayed from their ranks after departing the Panthéon and mingled with the crowds. Others left their ranks after standing about before the various *mairies*. There is no indication that any of these students took an active part in the fighting on the twenty-third, as the level of combat had diminished with the news of Guizot's departure from the government.[38]

Taking their lead from the committees that were meeting at *La Lanterne* and *L'Avant-Garde,* the more activist students met in the Place du Panthéon on the morning of the twenty-third. They could hear the gunfire coming from the Right Bank. Rather than build barricades in the Latin Quarter, where the National Guard was already antigovernment and where no fighting was in progress, the students decided to cross the river to join the ongoing struggle. Still unarmed, with perhaps the exception of a few who, as on the day before, kept their arms concealed, the students and others of the Left Bank marched several hundred strong toward the river singing the *Marseillaise.* Arriving before the entrance to the Pont Saint-Michel, they were stopped by units of the National Guard of the Eleventh Arrondissement. These loyal bourgeois supporters of the monarchy stood firm and refused to allow the students to pass over the bridge. A heated exchange took place. One student, who demanded that the guardsmen explain why the marchers were denied passage, was placed under arrest. When he resisted, he was struck in the face by a saber. The blow cut open the young man's lips.[39] His comrades, who were unarmed and thus had no hope of success in the event of a confrontation with the national guardsmen, remembered the age-old maxim: discretion is the better part of valor. They withdrew from the bridge and split into small groups of two or three. In this inconspicuous manner they made their way across the river and took part in the fighting and the demonstrations of the day.

While fighting was taking place in some northern quarters of the city during the early afternoon of the twenty-third, large antigovernment demonstrations were taking place along the boulevards. Following one of these demonstrations in the northeast part of Paris, about two thousand persons, most of them youths, gathered in the vicinity of the Place de la Bastille. At about 4 P.M. they received news that Guizot had been asked to resign and that the king was prepared to accept a more moderate government. The implication was that the people would get what they wanted. In the Place de la Bastille the soldiers and the young people fraternized as though the rebellion had ended. Then, with a small group of students from the Ecole Polytechnique and from the law and medical schools at the head, the crowd marched toward the river and the Latin Quarter beyond with the intention of fraternizing with the students who were manning a small number of hastily erected barricades in the vicinity of the schools.

The marchers crossed the Pont d'Austerlitz singing the *Marseillaise.* As they entered the rue des Fosses-Saint-Bernard, near the wine market, they came face to face with a unit of the Municipal Guard that had quickly formed ranks to prevent their passage. Before any words could be exchanged and without provocation on the part of the marchers, the guardsmen opened fire upon the young people. Ten marchers fell to the street as their comrades scattered for shelter. Only one volley was fired, yet three lay dead and seven were seriously wounded. The wounded, none of whom was a student, were taken to the hospital of the Pitié while their comrades spread the word that the rebellion had not ended.[40]

References to the combat role of the Parisian students are all too frequently given in vague and general terms. Certainly one aspect of the problem of assessing student participation is determining which young men were students and which were not. The *polytechniciens* were quickly recognized by their uniforms, but law, medical, or other students were not so readily identified. Their dress and their age were the best means of recognition, but certainly not infallible. The American student Charles Leland described how he was dressed while fighting on the barricades: "I was armed with dirk and pistols, wore a sash, and was unmistakably a Latin Quarter *étudiant,* as shown by long hair, rakish cap on one side, red neck-tie, and single eye-glass."[41]

There is no way to determine precisely how many students took part in the fighting on February 23 — or on February 24, for that matter. Surely only a small percentage of the student population of Paris participated. It should further be noted that, of the nearly dozen students who were wounded or killed during the February Days, at least one may not have been taking part in the fighting. On the morning of the twenty-third Louis-Charles Canda, a student at the Collège Louis-le-Grand, was shot in the head and killed at a barricade in the rue Planche-Mibray. Young Canda had been living with his parents at 10, rue de Port Royal while attending school. According to a report filed on April 23, 1848, with the Commission des blessés de février 1848, Canda "left his home on February 23 without having told his parents that he intended to take part in the fighting" and he was accidentally killed at the barricade. The boy's parents appear to be the source of this information, and the government investigator seems to have been satisfied that it was true.[42] Canda may have been an innocent bystander, but it is also possible that he had decided to

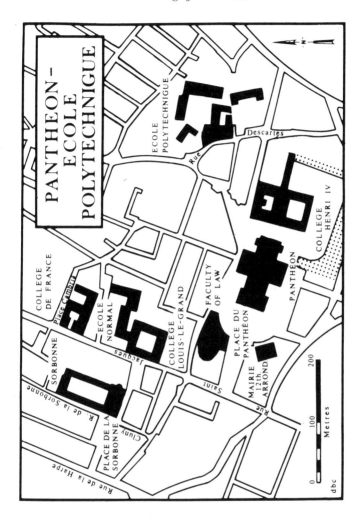

join the struggle without telling his parents. In either case, his death was officially listed as accidental.

A second student killed in the fighting on February 23 was Thomas Carrère. Carrère had been a teacher at the collège Royal de Versailles. He was married and had a two-year-old son. He had given up teaching in 1845 and had entered the medical school in Paris. He was wounded while "taking part in the national struggle" and was taken at once to the Hôtel-Dieu, where he was placed in bed number seven. Four days later, on February 27, Carrère died of his wound. His widow applied for and received a pension from the state.[43]

Other students, among them Charles Bellan and Edouard M. Commelin, fought in various parts of the city on the twenty-third. Bellan roamed the Right Bank seeking out the fighting. In the morning he was at a barricade in the rue Saint-Denis. However, as there was no fighting in progress, he went first to the rue du Bourg l'Abbé and then to the Hôtel de Ville. That night he assisted in the construction of barricades at the Porte Saint-Martin. The following morning he fought at the Palais-Royal.[44] Commelin fought at the barricades at the Place du Châtelet.[45]

The dismissal of Guizot brought the fighting in Paris to a near stop. There was rejoicing in some parts of the city and victory was proclaimed. Yet the workers were skeptical about the apparent concession on the part of the Bourgeois Monarchy. The older men remembered the "victory" on the barricades in July, 1830, a victory that in their view gave them nothing. Their working and living conditions had improved little in the eighteen years that had elapsed. Thus the workers and artisans did not dismantle their barricades; rather, they took a watch-and-wait attitude. Then came the news that Louis M. Molé had been asked to form a government. Count Molé, known to be a "constitutional moderate," represented a concession on the part of Louis Philippe to the parliamentarian Left. However, the workers saw in Molé a continuation of the same political, social, and economic regime. As darkness fell upon the city there was uncertainty and confusion: Was the rebellion over, or had it achieved only insignificant gains? Should the fighting be continued in the streets, or in the Chamber of Deputies? A massacre on the Boulevard des Capucines before the Ministry of Foreign Affairs answered these questions.

Early in the evening of February 23 a group of demonstrators was marching down the Boulevard des Capucines coming from the Faubourg Saint-Antoine. The group's mood was a mixture of satisfaction that the government had made concessions and displeasure as to the limitation of those concessions. For the first time in the February Days some of the demonstrators were carrying red flags, the symbol of the workers. As they approached the Ministry of Foreign Affairs, they came face to face with a unit of the Fourteenth Regiment of the line that was standing guard. Who fired the first shot has never been determined. It could have been the accidental discharge of a musket by a nervous soldier. It could have come from an armed demonstrator. Whatever its origin, the result was disastrous and decisive. The uneasy troops believed that they had been fired upon and they answered with a volley that killed more than forty persons and that wounded an equal number.

In this crowd was a self-styled "observer," M. Levasseur, a former student of the Collège Bourbon and at the time attending the Institut Boutet. Levasseur related the following: "I heard the firing of muskets and the whistling of the balls. A young man who was about to light his cigarette from mine fell on my shoulder, most likely wounded. I took to my heels in a bent-over position so as to avoid the balls that flew over head and was carried along in the wave of fugitives."[46] The demonstrators scattered in panic to seek safety. Then, after the troops had withdrawn, they returned to claim their dead. Some of the bodies were placed upon wagons and taken throughout the city in a torchlight procession.

Some contemporaries and, later, historians maintained that the dismissal of Guizot, together with the constitutional and political concessions that the appointment of Molé implied, was sufficient to bring an end to the February Days without the abdication of Louis Philippe. Others believed that he was no longer in control of the situation and that the monarchy was doomed. Both points of view become academic and incidental in light of the massacre on the Boulevard des Capucines. The joy that had been generated by the news of Guizot's dismissal disappeared as the torchlit wagons passed. No longer would Parisians be satisfied with political reform of the monarchy. What had started as a reform movement and had developed into a massive demonstration now became a full-scale revolution. The cries of "Long Live Reform!" were quickly replaced by even louder shouts of "Long live the Republic!"

By the night of February 23 the office of *L'Avant-Garde*, across from the Odéon theater at 5, rue Corneille, had become the center for student-organized activities. Several days before the scheduled banquet of February 22 the *Comité central des écoles* ("Central Committee of the Schools") had been formed by the schools in order to coordinate the activities of the students. The committee was made up of sixty elected members from the various schools of Paris. Whereas it is true that only a small percentage of students took part in the selection of its members, this committee was the most representative of any that the students of Paris brought into existence during those troubled days. The members of the old committee led by Watripon, although they were a minority within the *Comité central des écoles,* dominated the new committee. It was not until the evening of the twenty-third that the central committee, using the office of *L'Avant-Garde,* functioned with any effectiveness. Furthermore, the committee's influence was limited. It extended only to the immediate vicinity of the schools in the Latin Quarter, and even then it took at best the form of persuasive argument or general suggestion for action. Each individual barricade was completely autonomous and was governed by a very loose form of "democracy." However imperfect the central committee, it was the principal effort on the part of the students to organize themselves.[47]

News of the massacre on the Boulevard des Capucines spread rapidly while the night was still young. At the office of *L'Avant-Garde,* where the news was brought by a young man named Lagrange, a critical decision was made by the members of the central committee who happened to be present. The students realized at once that the tragedy would lead to full-scale revolution and that the tempo of fighting, which had been moderate on the twenty-third, would be greatly accelerated on the morning of the twenty-fourth. No longer could anyone participate effectively in the struggle without being armed. Therefore, small groups of students were sent out into the city to search for arms while others spent the night making powder and balls for the fighting that all were now sure would take place in the morning.[48] Two students, MM. Dessus and Bilbao, were given two or three firearms by Edgar Quinet when they appeared at his home and requested them.[49]

In another isolated incident a group of students broke into the bell tower of the church of Saint-Sulpice shortly before midnight. When the tower keeper demanded an explanation he was told that any moment the people would attack and "butcher the National Guard." The students, in order to prevent such a bloodbath, rang the bells for five minutes as a general alarm. They then occupied the church for the remainder of the night.[50]

.III.

The Rebellion Becomes
a Revolution: February 24

On the morning of February 24 those students of Paris
who enthusiastically had taken up the cause of reform
found themselves involved in a revolution to overthrow
the monarchy and to replace it with a republic. After the
massacre on the Boulevard des Capucines, few students
were willing to continue to support the king. The more
radical students, particularly those from the law and
medical schools, had been republicans before the February Days had begun. The students had desired—and
now demanded—constitutional reform and the independence of the schools from government control; if the
road led first to a republic they were prepared to follow it.
Furthermore, acceptable alternatives seemed to have
vanished by the morning of the twenty-fourth. A polarization of political thought that had taken place during
the preceding forty-eight hours was crystallized with the
news of the catastrophe on the Boulevard des Capucines.

There appeared to be only two choices: to support the
monarchy or to defend the barricades. The former implied the maintenance of the status quo and the approval
of the massacre; the latter, it was presumed, would lead to
a republic and to reform. The students had little difficulty in making their choice. A Louis Molé or an Adolphe
Thiers might extend the franchise or allow greater freedom of association and thus pacify the dynastic opposition, but would he liberalize the government's firm control of the university community by granting greater
academic freedom to faculty and students? The students

were skeptical. However, the possibility of a republic—
which only the more radical had dreamed of two days
earlier—now raised before their eyes visions of a new
France that would be in harmony with the younger generation. The students were not fundamentally republicans. Furthermore, like their bourgeois parents, they
feared a revival of Jacobinism of the 1793–94 style. When
they accepted republicanism in February, 1848, they
thought more of the moderate Girdondins than of the
social and economic "radicalism" of Robespierre, Saint-
Just, and Couthon. Thus those students of Paris who
went to the barricades on February 24 did so with the
same zeal and expectation with which the workers and
artisans would go in June.

News of the massacre on the Boulevard des Capucines
had reached the Tuileries about ten o'clock on the evening of the twenty-third. Molé, who had been trying
desperately to form a government since late in the afternoon, informed the king at midnight that the course of
events had rendered his task impossible. Thereupon,
Louis Philippe sent for Adolphe Thiers. Thiers, a leading
figure in the parliamentary opposition, agreed to form a
cabinet with the understanding that Odilon Barrot, who
was much despised by the king for his liberalism, be part
of the government. Thiers quite incorrectly believed that
he and Barrot were popular enough with the masses in
Paris to enable them to end the rebellion and to form a
"liberal" cabinet. However, after the two men had hur-
ried from barricade to barricade throughout the early
hours of the twenty-fourth, Thiers returned to the
Tuileries at 8 A.M., dirty and smelling of gunpowder, to
inform the bewildered king that given the mood of Paris
it was his opinion that only Barrot could form a government acceptable to the people who manned the barricades.

While Thiers and Barrot were attempting to talk the
Parisians out of their barricades, the government was
making preparations to blast them out. Louis Philippe
had reluctantly appointed General Thomas R. Bugeaud,
a veteran of the North African wars, as commander of all

troops in and about Paris and had charged him with the responsibility of restoring order in the streets. Bugeaud immediately held a council of war and informed his subordinates of his master plan for accomplishing the objective. He had, he believed, the necessary troop strength: on paper his command consisted of 36,000 soldiers, 3,200 men of the Municipal Guard, and the National Guard. But for the operations on the twenty-fourth he could actually muster only 16,000 troops, the Municipal Guard, and the unreliable National Guard.[1] Bugeaud was aware that the civilian guardsmen were of questionable value and might be of no help to him, but he discounted the importance of their loyalty and planned to regain control of the city with or without their support. His plan was simple and straightforward. Four columns were to be formed of the troops that were gathered in the vicinity of the Tuileries. The first, commanded by General Marie-Alphonse Bedeau, would make its way to the Place de la Bastille by way of the Grands Boulevards, while the second, commanded by General Tiburce Sebastiani, marched to the Hôtel de Ville and then on to the Banque de France. A third force was to secure the rear of the first two. The fourth column, under Colonel Jean-André-Louis Brunet, would cross the Seine and march to the Panthéon.

Of the four columns, only Colonel Brunet's accomplished its objective. General Bedeau bogged down on the Boulevard Poisonnière and General Sebastiani got only so far as the Hôtel de Ville. Their supporting force had little to secure. But Colonel Brunet marched his troops across the Seine to the rue Saint-Pères and then via the rues Jacob, de la Seine, de Tournon, the Place Saint-Michel, and the rue Saint-Dominique to the Panthéon.[2] He encountered no barricades along the way as the center of resistance on the Left Bank was east of his line of march. Brunet's troops, which reinforced those of General Renault already at the Panthéon, remained inactive throughout the morning in the shadow of that magnificant structure.

Back at the Tuileries, Bugeaud, who was receiving

discouraging and conflicting reports, began to waver. First Bedeau and then Sebastiani were ordered to cease hostilities and to fall back to the vicinity of the Tuileries. The National Guard was to assume responsibility for maintaining order. This action was taken to prevent the enormous loss of life that would have occurred in the event of a head-on collision of the troops and the defenders of the barricades. Furthermore, the soldiers had shown signs of being unhappy with their assigned role when they were confronted by the people of Paris. A number of Sebastiani's men, as they stood idly before the Hôtel de Ville, had been disarmed by the rebels. Thus it was deemed expedient to separate the troops from the people before the army melted away. It was not that the army rank and file would not fire upon the barricades, but rather that the leadership was indecisive and reluctant to engage in full-scale battle with the civilian population of the city.

The morning of the twenty-fourth saw scattered fighting throughout Paris. The major "confrontations" took place on the Right Bank, with the fighting at Château d'eau being the most bloody. Most of the minor skirmishes were between the barricade defenders and the Municipal Guard or units of the National Guard. On the Left Bank the fighting was relatively light, as it had been the two previous days.

The majority of the barricades on the Left Bank were built in the narrow streets between the Panthéon and the river—that is, the area that included the Latin Quarter. They were constructed and manned by workers, artisans, lower bourgeoisie, and the students. Charles Leland, who spent the entire three days in the streets, declared, "There were very few gentlemen indeed among the insurgents. I only observed two or three in our quarter [the Latin Quarter] and they were all from our hotel.[3] But the next day every swell in Paris came out as an insurgent. *They* had all worked at barricades—so they said. I certainly had not seen any of them at work."[4] The barricade defenders generally lived in the immediate vicinity of the structure they manned. The barricades built and defended primarily by the students were near the schools in the Latin Quarter. These structures were made of paving stones, which were easily pried out of the sand that held them in place. To the stones was added whatever else was at hand—carriages, carts, iron grillworks, furniture, lumber, doors, and so on. Along the boulevards, along the quais of the Seine, and in other parts of the city where they were available, trees were cut down and used in the construction of barricades.

The strongest system of barricades on the Left Bank centered about the Carrefour Buci. All the streets leading into the *carrefour*—Bussi, Mazarine, Dauphine, Saint-André-des-Arts and l'Ancienne-Comédie—were barricaded. These formidable structures were defended by some four hundred men who were well supplied by the inhabitants of the area. Women and children helped in the preparations by littering the approaches to the barricades with broken glass. Only a handful of students took part in this operation, but the medical students from the faculty of medicine, which was close by, organized an ambulance service and set up first-aid stations. During the heavy fighting of the morning of the twenty-fourth the students treated the wounded as best they could in their makeshift hospitals.[5]

The fighting at Bussi was the heaviest on the Left Bank. Troops crossed the Pont Neuf and attempted to take the barricade in the rue Dauphine. But the withering fire from behind the stone barricade and the sniper fire from the windows above the street convinced the commanding officer that, even if he could carry the barricade, the price of victory would be prohibitive. He therefore broke off the engagement and fell back onto the Pont Neuf to take up a defensive position.[6] On the morning of the twenty-fourth the insurgents at Bussi proclaimed from their barricades the Second Republic. Their proclamation not only preceded that of the Chamber of Deputies by several hours, but also was made before the king had abdicated.

The rue Saint-Jacques, which runs through the center of the Latin Quarter and which in 1848 was the main

north-south artery on the Left Bank, was cut by nine
barricades between the river and the Panthéon. Several
of these barricades in the vicinity of the Sorbonne and the
Collège de France were defended by students and young
workers from the district. Directly in front of the office of
La Lanterne, at 98, rue Saint-Jacques, was a sturdy structure that measured ten feet in height and ten feet at its
base. On the morning of the twenty-fourth, a company of
municipal guardsmen advanced upon this barricade and,
firing a volley at its defenders, killed one student and
wounded another young man. The guardsmen expected
that the untrained and undisciplined civilians would flee
before this show of force. But the students and workers
who defended the barricade were both armed and determined, unlike the demonstrators who had been relatively easy to disperse on the preceding two days. They
returned the fire, killing and wounding several of the
advancing guardsmen. The formidable structure and the
determination of the defenders quickly convinced the
attackers that the price of victory would surely be too
costly. The guardsmen withdrew in good order, leaving
the rue Saint-Jacques to the insurgents.[7]

The National Guard of the 12th Arrondissement
posed no danger to the rebels in the Latin Quarter.
Because of his troops' antigovernment sentiments and
their refusal to take action against the insurgents on the
twenty-third, Colonel Lavocat, who had spent the night
at the *mairie,* decided not to call out his men on the
twenty-fourth. Lavocat, who had been appointed by the
Minister of the Interior, was not popular with the men he
commanded. Nevertheless, without his having given the
order, the drums calling the guardsmen to arms had been
beaten throughout the *arrondissement.*[8] The Twelfth Legion did not turn out in large numbers, but the men who
did gather in the Place du Panthéon were even more
violently opposed to the government than they had been
the previous morning. Lavocat, realizing immediately
that he had lost effective control of his men, gave up his
command and retired to his home.[9] Following the departure of the colonel the national guardsmen went over to

the side of the people and helped them to build barricades and instructed them in the use of firearms.[10]

The scene at the Ecole Polytechnique on the morning
of the twenty-fourth was similar to that on the previous
day. The students attended their first class amid much
talk of the role they had played in the events of the day
before. By 8 A.M. news of the massacre on the Boulevard
des Capucines had spread throughout the school and
had caused great agitation. Instead of going to their
study halls as scheduled, the students assembled in the
auditorium to discuss what action they should take in
light of the new developments. Paris was once again in a
state of turmoil and conflict. What role should the
polytechniciens play in this revolution? Tradition, however
poorly based on historical fact, would seem to ally them
with the people. After some discussion it was decided that
they would again divide themselves into small groups and
try to stop the senseless bloodshed so that some kind of
political arrangement, satisfactory to all concerned,
could be worked out.

Once again it is evident from their decision that the
polytechniciens were not politically involved in the February Days. Their neutral position, even after the violence of the night of the twenty-third, showed that
whereas they had their grievances with the established
order, moderate change within the framework of the
monarchy was the most they desired. Nor were they
unanimous even in this general view. There were
monarchists, both legitimists and Orleanists, and "liber-
als," not necessarily republicans, who opposed the decision of the majority. The former desired to remain within
the confines of the school while the latter wished to join
the people in their attack against the government.

The decision having been made to play an active but
neutral role in the struggle taking place throughout the
city, the students sent a delegation to inform the school's
commander, General Aupick, of their intentions. The
general, accompanied by his staff, went at once to the
auditorium. He asked his students not to leave the school,
but he took no action to prevent their departure. He

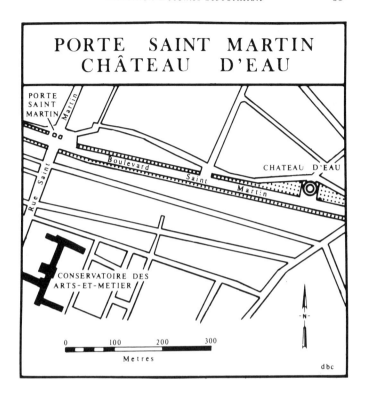

PORTE SAINT MARTIN
CHÂTEAU D'EAU

knew that they had arrived at a decision from which they would not retreat. He also knew that there was a menacing mob at the main gate demanding that the students come out and join it. The mob could not be held off indefinitely, and he feared for the life of his guards and his staff should it gain entrance. Thus General Aupick stood by and watched the *polytechniciens* march four by four, in full-dress uniforms complete with swords, out into the street.[11]

The people in the streets cheered loudly as the students marched towards the Place du Panthéon. The soldiers who guarded the entrances to the Place opened their ranks to allow the young men to pass and presented arms. When the *polytechniciens* arrived before the *mairie* of the Twelfth Arrondissement, they found a state of near anarchy. The national guardsmen were leaderless, the civil authority was without instructions, and the army, which had been receiving contradictory orders throughout the night and morning, was indecisive. After briefly consulting with the civil and military leaders at the *mairie*, the students divided themselves into small groups and departed for various parts of the city where they hoped, with the support of the National Guard, to stop the bloodshed. Although there were few reports of fighting on the Left Bank, they could hear the gunfire from the Saint-Denis and Château d'eau districts.[12]

The role played by the *polytechniciens* varied in accordance with the particular situation in which the different groups found themselves. In the Eleventh Arrondissement they calmed a crowd gathered before the *mairie*. The people were demanding arms and the mayor was stalling for time when the small group of students arrived on the scene. Upon the frantic urging of the mayor, one of the *polytechniciens* addressed the demonstrators: "Reform we will certainly have," he said, "but maintain your dignity by staying calm. Let your moderation be as distinguished as your courage."[13] These words were well received and the crowd answered with a lively shout of "Vive l'Ecole!" Impressed more by the youthful student in his elegant uniform than by his reasoning, however, the people were only temporarily appeased. It was the timely arrival of a messenger from the Tuileries that led to the dispersal of the crowd. He brought orders for the soldiers to hold their fire and to return to their barracks.

Across the river in the Eighth Arrondissement a somewhat different episode unfolded. Charles de Freycinet and a small group of fellow *polytechniciens* had crossed half of the city by the time they reached the military barracks in the rue Popincourt. There they found an angry mob demanding that the soldiers turn over their arms to the people. The arrival of the students, in their impressive and readily recognized uniforms, had a calming effect upon the gathering as a dialogue took place with the newcomers. During this interlude Freycinet gained entrance to the barracks and was given permission to speak to the colonel in command. The officer was both perplexed and desperate. He had received orders not to fire upon the people, and his dilemma was how to prevent the crowd in the street from forcing entrance and disarming his troops without disobeying his superiors. Freycinet provided a solution. The troops would leave the city taking their arms with them. Thus there would be neither bloodshed, surrender, nor loss of honor. The colonel agreed and Freycinet took his compromise to the people in the street. Although they had desired the arms that the troops possessed, they were convinced that they would get them only from dead soldiers. The solution proposed by the young student would at least rid the quarter of the troops and leave it entirely in the hands of the people. With the agreement of both sides the *polytechniciens* placed themselves at the head of the column and to the cheers of "Vive la ligne!" led the soldiers through the streets toward the suburbs. After seeing the column to safety in the vicinity of the Vincennes, the students returned to the Place de la Bastille. Upon their arrival in the Place they heard the news that the king had abdicated and that a provisional government was to be formed.[14]

The detachment of *polytechniciens* assigned to the First Arrondissement was accompanied by a dozen national

guardsmen and two drummers. As the small column
made its way across the Seine and along the quai, it was
joined by an increasing number of people until it comprised hundreds. As they marched along, the people
began to plunder munitions shops and to shout pro-
fanities against Guizot. They came upon a group led by a
man carrying a red flag. The student sergeant who
headed the *polytechniciens* confronted the flag bearer and
declared in a firm tone that he wanted no other flag to fly
except the Tricolor. The red flag was at once taken and
torn into pieces. The column continued to the Place de la
Concorde. It crossed the Place to the rue Royale, where
workers told the students that an attack on the military
barracks in the rue Penthièvre was imminent. The
sergeant rushed to the scene with his comrades, arriving
just as the large mob was beginning its attack. The student sergeant climbed atop a large stone and addressed
the would-be assailants. The barracks was manned by
brave French soldiers, he declared, whose tradition and
honor would not allow them to give up their arms as the
people desired. Then he added a more convincing argument: the people would undoubtedly be calling upon
these same brave men to defend them against foreign
despots when the revolution was successful. The people
responded to these elegant words with shouts of "Vive
l'Ecole Polytechnique! Vive l'armée!"[15] The crowd then
moved on, leaving the soldiers in peace.

The police barracks in the rue des Francs-Bourgeois in
the Seventh Arrondissement was threatened late on the
morning of the twenty-fourth. The angry crowd
gathered before the barracks demanded that it be given
the arms of the men inside. The spokesman for the
people was Pasteur d'Etreillis, a captain in the National
Guard. D'Etreillis, accompanied by a student from the
Ecole Polytechnique and a barricade defender from the
nearby *carrefour* of the rues Vieille Temple, de Paradis,
and des Francs-Bourgeois, gained entrance to negotiate
with the besieged officers. An arrangement was agreed
upon by which the people would be given the arms from
the barracks but would not be allowed entry. Two na-

tional guardsmen and the *polytechniciens* remained inside
to ensure that the barracks would not be attacked after it
had been disarmed.[16] The people, satisfied that they had
acquired arms and neutralized the officers, departed.

Shortly after the *polytechniciens* assigned to the Ninth
Arrondissement reached the *mairie,* several of them
agreed to act as *aides de camp* to Captain Necolas Antoine
Jourdan. Jourdan was an energetic National Guard officer whose willingness to assume command and whose
ability to make quick decisions caused him to stand out
from his colleagues. When the sounds of gunfire were
heard coming from the nearby Place de la Bastille, Jourdan and three of his new *aides de camp,* MM. Augier, Astie,
and Requin, rushed to the trouble spot. With the aid of
the three students and Wilfried de Fonvielle, who had
marched with them from the Place du Panthéon, the
fighting was quickly stopped.[17]

Not every *polytechnicien* played a neutral role in accordance with the decision of that eventful morning. No real
pattern emerges although, in general, the majority acted
as did the national guardsmen with whom they were
closely associated. But some acted independently of the
National Guard and fought with or led the people against
the troops.

Two *polytechniciens,* having placed themselves at the
head of a large menacing band of insurgents, led the
people into a military barracks in the Fourth Arrondissement. The soldiers allowed themselves to be disarmed and the munitions from the storage rooms to be
carried away. The National Guard company at the scene
stood by idly.[18]

In the Eleventh Arrondissement the group of students
who had marched over from the Place du Panthéon
attached themselves to the Eleventh Legion of the National Guard. Thus when this National Guard unit, which
was one of the most loyal to the monarchy, attacked the
great barricade in the rue du Cherche-Midi, the *polytechniciens* fought against the people. After the defenders
had been driven away, the guardsmen and the students
occupied the nearby prison and put the prisoners, who

had been released by the people, back into their cells. They also put out fires that had been started.[19]

Other *polytechniciens* played a more independent and active role. One of these young men, whose name has eluded history, commanded a barricade in the heart of the Latin Quarter. When the defenders were attacked by troops of the line, this eighteen-year-old student climbed to the top of the barricade and, wrapping himself in the Tricolor, called out to the soldiers, "Now I defy you to shoot!" The troops, who were not enthusiastic in their defense of the unpopular monarchy, held their fire and withdrew.[20]

While the students were spread over the entire city in small groups, there was trouble back at the Ecole Polytechnique. The streets about the school, especially the rues de la Montagne Sainte-Geneviève, and Descartes, were barricaded. In mid-morning General Renault, at the head of a company of the Fifty-fifth Regiment, attacked the barricades in front of the school and cleared them of insurgents. Leaving a small detachment, which he later reinforced, to hold the immediate area, he retired to the Place du Panthéon. The soldiers, under the command of Captain Beaulaincourt, took up a position before the school as the insurgents threateningly rebuilt their barricades. The people began to fraternize with the soldiers and to give them food and wine. But then there rang out a shot, which led both sides to believe that the other had started fighting. Lepelletier Roinville states that the fighting broke out when a drunken civilian fired his weapon at the soldiers.[21] More shots forced the people to flee for the safety of nearby houses and barricades. The troops took up a battle formation, but the gunfire from the windows of adjacent buildings and from the barricades forced Beaulaincourt and his men to take refuge within the walls of the Ecole Polytechnique. As the soldiers reached the central courtyard of the school the insurgents pressed hard upon their heels. It was only through the efforts of General Aupick, his staff, and a few students who had returned (one of them named Jacquier) that the school and the troops were spared.[22] The insurgents threatened Aupick's life and were placated only when the students explained that he was "their" general and that they wanted no harm to come to him.[23]

Casualties had been heavy on both sides. In the course of the fighting before the Ecole Polytechnique a medical student, Eugène Curie, who was with the attacking insurgents, was seriously wounded by a musket ball. He was taken to the hospital of the Pitié, where his wound was treated.[24]

The officers of Beaulaincourt's command changed into civilian clothes and were then escorted by an employee of the school back to their barracks in the rue des Bourguignons. The soldiers had remained in the school's central courtyard until after dark. About 9 P.M. they had been led out through a little-used side door and General Aupick had posted a student guard at the two main gates of the school.[25]

In other fighting near the Sorbonne an architectural student, eighteen-year-old Oscar Robin, was wounded. Robin was on the barricade at the Place Cambria (now a part of the Place Marcilin Berthel before the Collège de France) when it was attacked by a unit of the Municipal Guard about 10 A.M. the twenty-fourth. He was struck just below the right shoulder by a musket ball and was carried from the barricade. His wound was cared for with skill sufficient to save his life.[26]

While Captain Jourdan and his student *aides de camp* were preventing bloodshed at the Place de la Bastille, Victor Hugo, accompanied by his two sons, was in the Place du Palais-Royal trying desperately, but unsuccessfully, to calm a large crowd that was bent on marching to the Hôtel de Ville. As he was atempting to reason with the people, several *polytechniciens* entered the Place. Hugo called them forward and implored one of the students to speak to the people and to calm them. The young man addressed the crowd but his words were to no avail. Realizing that it was too late for words, his comrades put themselves at the head of the people and led the march toward the Hôtel de Ville.[27]

The *polytechniciens*, with their elegant uniforms and
swords, stood out from the crowds on February 24.
Wherever they went they were immediately recognized
as students. Their popularity was nearly universal. The
army, the National Guard, the workers and artisans in
the street, and the bourgeois shopkeepers—all admired
and respected the *polytechnicien* and looked upon him as
the future servant of the state. Indeed, from the two
classes of the Ecole Polytechnique that took part in the
February Days (the entering classes of 1846 and 1847)
there emerged thirteen generals and an impressive array
of inspector generals of roads, bridges, and mines.[28]
Eyewitness accounts and memoirs of contemporaries
contain many references to those particular *polytechniciens*.

The same is not true for other students who played an
active role in the revolution of 1848. A law or medical
student was not instantly recognized as such. One might
know by his dress and his speech that he was not a worker
or an artisan, but there was no assurance that he was a
student. The terms "young people" and "young people
of the Quarter" are frequently found in contemporary
accounts. Such terms may, and when used in reference to
groups in the Twelfth Arrondissement most likely do,
include students. The most specific references to students are to be found in the casualty lists of the *procès-
verbaux* ("official reports") from the various quarters of
Paris, in the files of the Commission des blessés de février
1848, and in the dossiers of the police archives.

Eustice Philippe Jacquier was a twenty-four-year-old
medical student who fought and was wounded in the
February Days. By his own admission he was a republican
before the revolution. On the twenty-second he joined
the students who marched from the Panthéon and
played an active role in the fight on that first day. During
the three days of fighting he did care for some of the
wounded but his principal role was that of a combatant.
On the twenty-fourth Jacquier was seriously wounded in
the back by a musket ball.[29]

The bloodiest confrontation on the February Days was

fought on the morning of the twenty-fourth between insurgents and troops of the line of Château d'eau. Strategically situated as it was—it became the focal point in the struggle to control the center of Paris. Fighting broke out when insurgents attempted to disarm troops stationed before the structure in the Place du Palais-Royal. Who fired the first shot remains a mystery despite numerous eyewitness accounts. But the fighting that ensued was desperate on both sides. Aleide Joseph Victor Reynard, a law student, took part in this fighting. The son of a well-to-do Parisian bourgeois, young Reynard had commanded a barricade during the early morning of the twenty-fourth in the Faubourg Montmarte. As the heavier fighting developed in the center of the city, he followed the sounds of the guns to Château d'eau. While taking part in the fighting there, his foot was injured by stones falling from one of the barricades. His injury was attended by Dr. France, a member of the faculty of medicine, and gradually Reynard regained full use of the foot.[30]

Charles Stoffel, a twenty-eight-year-old student from Strasbourg, was also wounded in the fighting at Château d'eau. Stoffel received 950 francs over a seven-year period for a wound he received on his right hand.[31] Two other students also took part in the struggle at Château d'eau: Dehon Remy,[32] a twenty-three-year-old student at the Ecole de Pharmacie ("College of Pharmacy"), and Louis Redon,[33] a thirty-one-year-old law student. Redon had also fought at the barricades on the rues de Beaubourg and Rambuteau. A medical student, Auguste Corlieu, helped care for the wounded at Château d'eau "with many doctors and [medical] students."[34]

Positive identifications can be made of two other students injured while manning barricades on the twenty-fourth. A law student, M. Dauvet, who lived at 8, rue de Cluny, was injured when he fell from the top of a barricade at the medical school.[35] A second law student, M. Stoffel, who lived at 95, rue Saint-Jacques, was "lightly wounded on the hand."[36] No indication is given in the police report as to where the latter incident took place.

A student from the Collège Colbert, Jean Paul Guer-reau, only fourteen years of age, was killed by musket fire from the Municipal Guard. The boy was struck as he was crossing the rue Saint-Honoré near his home. His father later declared that young Guerreau was on his way to his father's place of business when the accident occurred.[37]

The dossiers in the police archives identify five other students: Joseph Ubel, twenty-three, fought at the Palais-Royal on the twenty-fourth;[38] two students from the College of Pharmacy, Charles Greppo, twenty-two, and Etienne F. Boussard, twenty-six, also fought on the barricades;[39] and seventeen-year-old Henri A. Martin commanded a barricade in the rue Vieille Temple during the fighting on the twenty-fourth.[40] At the Préfecture de Police a twenty-nine-year-old law student, Fulgeme Ma-nin, was responsible for the bloodless occupation of the building in the early afternoon of the twenty-fourth. He persuaded the troops guarding the prefecture to with-draw and to allow the people to occupy the structure.[41]

In the lists of killed and wounded only one man is identified as a teacher. A twenty-eight-year-old professor of mathematics, G. Raincourt, was wounded in the fight-ing during the February Days. As a result of his wound he made fifteen visits to the doctor (at 5 francs per visit) and spent 120 francs on medicine and 10 francs on transpor-tation. He later asked the government to reimburse him 310 francs.[42] The dossier of Joannis Guigard verifies the active particiaption of this thirty-two-year-old professor of mathematics in the February fighting. A member of the Société des droits d l'homme ("Society of the Rights of Man"), Guigard was a graduate of the Ecole Poly-technique, class of 1844.[43]

The medical students from the military hospital Val-de-Grace played a very active role in the last two days of fighting. Some tended the wounded, both civilian as well as military, who were brought to the hospital, while others went out into the city and gave first-aid treatment to the wounded under fire.[44]

The course of events moved swiftly on February 24. At

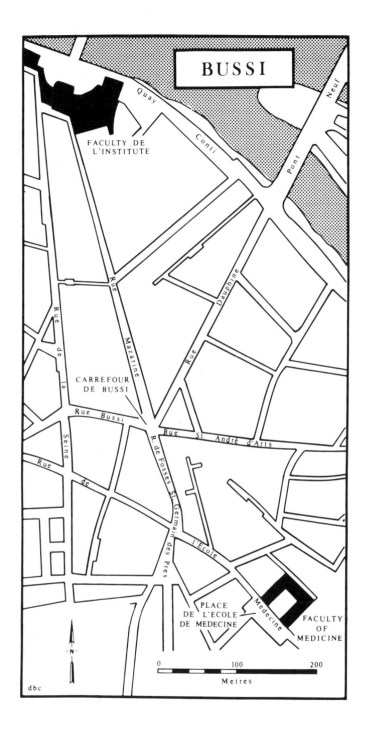

BUSSI

Quay Conti

Pont Neuf

FACULTY DE
L'INSTITUTE

Rue Mazarine

Rue Dauphine

CARREFOUR
DE BUSSI

Rue Bussi

Rue de la Seine

Rue de

R. de Fosses St. Germain des Pres

Rue St. André d'Arts

l'Ecole

Medecine

PLACE
DE L'ECOLE
DE MEDECINE

FACULTY
OF
MEDICINE

N

0   100   200

Metres

dbc

the Tuileries, Louis Philippe, realizing that the situation had become extremely serious by 10 A.M., decided to make one last attempt to reverse the rising tide that was threatening to engulf the monarchy. Wearing the uniform of a general, and accompanied by two of his sons and General Bugeaud, the king set out to review and rally the troops and the National Guard units that were in the gardens of the Tuileries and in the Place de la Concorde. Although the guardsmen of the First and Tenth legions received him cordially, the men of the Fourth greeted their monarch with loud cries of "Vive la Réforme!" The king lost heart. If these were the men called upon to defend his throne, there was indeed little hope of surviving the crisis.

Louis Philippe returned to the Tuileries and decided to abdicate. Rather than leave the throne vacant, he abdicated in favor of his grandson, the Count of Paris, and named his daughter-in-law, Hélene, the Duchess of Orleans, as regent. Then, dressed as a common citizen, he hastily departed for Le Havre, whence he sailed to England.

In Paris the course of the revolution was still uncertain. The Chamber of Deputies opened its regularly scheduled meeting about 3 P.M. amid great confusion. The republicans had spent the day preparing for the meeting. The editors and the supporters of the two influential journals of the Left, *La Réforme* and *Le National,* had made an uneasy alliance, the aim of which was to set up a provisional government for a second French republic. At the last minute they won over the popular and influential poet and author, Alphonse de Lamartine. The only hope for the Orleanists was the duchess and her ten-year-old son, both of whom presented themselves at the Palais-Bourbon. Their efforts were to no avail. The fate of the monarchy hung in the balance during the first speeches made to the deputies; but Lamartine, addressing himself to a Chamber that had been overrun by hostile insurgents, put the finishing touch to the July Monarchy. He called for the creation of a provisional government and threw in his lot with the republicans. Shortly thereafter seven representatives from the Chamber of Deputies made their way to the Hôtel de Ville for the purpose of establishing a provisional government and proclaiming a republic.

Following the departure of the king from the Tuileries shortly after noon, the insurgents forced their way into the palace. The mob was intent upon plunder and destruction, and it wreaked havoc upon the furnishings and interior of the palace. Only the chapel was temporarily spared. A student from the Ecole Polytechnique, M. Perreau, rushed forward and removed the blessed sacrament from the altar. Escorted by several of his comrades, he took his revered treasure to the church of Saint-Roch in the nearby rue Saint-Honoré.[45]

The same fate that befell the Tuileries might well have been in store for the old palace of the Louvre but for the intervention of several *polytechniciens*. Percy B. St. John, an Englishman residing in Paris at the time of the revolution, provides the following account: "Having watched awhile the disposition of the mighty populace at the Tuileries. . . . I traversed rapidly the other apartments, and entered the gallery of the Louvre, comparatively empty, save where a few Polytechnic students moved about as guardians of the nation's property."[46] Through the actions of these students the Louvre was spared.

At the nearby Palais-Royal another attempt was being made to prevent the destruction of valuable art objects. Maxime Du Camp was pleading unsuccessfully with a mob bent on plunder and destruction when a *polytechnicien* happened onto the scene. Du Camp hailed the student and ordered him to do something to stop the pillage. "The poor young man heard me without understanding what I was saying," Du Camp wrote in his memoirs. "Finally he raised his arms in a gesture of discouragement and said to me: 'What do you want me to do about it?' The mob continued its ignoble work."[47]

A small group of earnest men gathered at the Hôtel de Ville determined to put together a provisional government to fill the void created by the overthrow of the monarchy. Led by Lamartine, and including republicans (such as Jacques-Charles Dupont de l'Eure), socialists (such as Louis Blanc and Ferdinand Floçon), and a worker (Alexandre Martin, better known as "Albert"), the group labored throughout the night of February 24-25. Despite numerous interruptions by delegations, which were continually being sent inside by the vast multitude gathered in the square before the Hôtel de Ville, and despite near unresolvable differences among the leaders within, an eleven-man Provisional Government of the Republic was at last acclaimed by the people.

A number of *polytechniciens* had gained entrance to the Hôtel de Ville late on the afternoon of the twenty-fourth. Some of these young men had come with Captain Jourdan from the Place de la Bastille. Others had arrived from the Place du Palais-Royal at the head of a band of insurgents. Still others had drifted to the symbol of authority as the fighting died down throughout the city. As the Provisional Government was taking shape, the students offered their services as messengers. Their offer was accepted and the *polytechniciens*, in uniform as always, could be easily identified as they dashed about the city in their new official capacity.[48]

The excitement of February 24 subsided only gradually in the early hours of February 25. The army and the Municipal Guard had withdrawn into their barracks or had left the city. The National Guard patrolled the still noisy streets through which mobs of celebrants roamed, more frequently than not under the influence of alcohol. In many parts of the city men waited at their barricades for news of events at the Chamber of Deputies and later from the Hôtel de Ville. There was much talk among the workers and artisans of how they had won on the barricades. They also expressed mistrust of the men who were forming the Provisional Government. Only the proclamation of the Republic and the announcement of the members of the Provisional Government set them somewhat at ease.

The students, for their part, were pleased with the outcome of the "Glorious Three Days." Their aim on February 22 had not been the overthrow of the monar-

chy, but they felt no regrets when it fell and were generally satisfied with the proclamation of the Republic. They
seemed to feel confident that the new government would
put to right the wrongs of the monarchy, and that the
conditions of the academic community would be improved. They had no interest in changing either the
social or the economic structure of the nation. Their
sympathy for the poorer classes was general and philan-
thropic: it was unfortunate that people were poor and
miserable, but if they worked hard and lived prudently
they would surely rise above their squalor; the role of
government was to provide the tranquility and freedom
that were necessary for the academic—and the
business—community to thrive. These bourgeois attitudes would govern the actions of the students
throughout the spring of 1848; but even more important
they would determine the students' action—or perhaps it
should be said, their *inaction*—during the June Days.

.IV.

The Students and the
Provisional Government

On the morning of February 25 many of the students of Paris met at their favorite cafes to discuss the recent events and to relate their experiences of the past days. Classes did not resume until the following week, by which time Paris had begun to calm down.[1] The bloodshed had come to an end but Paris was in shambles. More than fourteen hundred barricades still stood throughout the city. Many of them had been manned throughout the night of the twenty-fourth as the workers awaited news that their victory in the streets had been confirmed by victory at the Hôtel de Ville. The newly created Provisional Government of the Republic could not ignore their presence or their demands. The proclamation of a republic, the declaration of the right to work, the establishment of the Luxembourg Commission with Louis Blanc at its head, and the creation of the national workshops followed in rapid succession. These measures were designed to appease the working classes and for a short time they succeeded. But the most pressing problems on the twenty-fifth were the restoration of normality in the city of Paris and the dispatching of the revolution to the provinces.

The students of the Ecole Polytechnique were again conspicuous in the days that followed the fighting. Those who became *aides de camp* to the Provisional Government were named in a special order signed by Alexandre Marie, the new minister of the interior, and by Dupont de l'Eure, the president of the Provisional Government.

Charles de Freycinet's name headed the list of students and was followed by those of fifteen of his comrades.[2] These young men escorted and "protected" the members of the Provisional Government during the first forty-eight hours of the new regime, which were marked by a mixture of celebration, plundering, and destruction. They were also seen darting about the city carrying orders and instructions to the ministries and the *mairies*.

Other *polytechniciens* helped to restore order in various quarters of the city. At the Orléans and Rouen (St. Lazare) railroad stations, with the support of other students, they were influential in preventing mobs from ransacking the stations and trains.[3] At the Lourcine military barracks they prevented a mob from looting the arms and munitions stored there. One *polytechnicien,* "citizen Servient," was named "Commander of the Louvre" by the Provisional Government after he had been chosen by his comrades.[4] The *polytechniciens* also worked in the streets to remove barricades and to restore circulation and communication.[5]

One group of students went each morning to General Guegnard, commander of the National Guard, and placed themselves at his disposal. These young men accompanied National Guard units about the city by day and made the rounds of the National Guard posts at night to make sure that all was well. Five or six *polytechniciens* went to the Tuileries and, entering the departed king's apartment, went through his private papers and correspondence that had been saved from the wrath of the people. They destroyed those documents they deemed incriminating and preserved those they considered harmless.[6] Still another group of students carried the royal jewels to a safe place where they would not fall into the hands of the plundering mobs that continued to sack the Tuileries and roam Paris.[7]

On February 24 most of the soldiers stationed in Paris had returned to their barracks, where they spent the night. Others had left the city. Some of those remaining had been disarmed but the presence of the large number of troops still in Paris on February 25 was considered

threatening by the working classes and undesirable by
the new government, which could not yet be sure of the
loyalty of the troops. Therefore, the *polytechniciens* undertook the task of escorting the troops from their barracks
to points outside the city. Each batallion had at its head
several students as it marched through the streets toward
the suburbs.

An order dated February 25 called upon the *polytechniciens* to assist in restoring the normal flow of food to the
people of Paris: "The students of the Ecole Polytechnique and the citizens Bassano and Solms are charged
with full powers to execute the orders issued by the
Provisional Government of the Republic for the provi-
sion of food."[8] This order, which was signed by all the
members of the Provisional Government, was important
because the development of a food shortage in the capital
would have led immediately to protest demonstrations, if
not riots, against the government and would have
weakened its position. Late on the afternoon of the
twenty-fifth, C. J. Madeleine Loir, a second-year student,
was sent out from the Hôtel de Ville with a stick measur-
ing two and one-half meters in length. His instructions
were to go to all the barricades on the rue Saint-Martin
from the center of the city to the Faubourg Saint-Martin
and to open a section of each structure so that food
wagons could reach the inner city on the morning of the
twenty-sixth. Loir accomplished this task in the pouring
rain with a minimum of difficulty. The commander of
one barricade at first resisted but gave way to reason in
the end. Loir returned to the Hôtel de Ville at 2 A.M. to
announce the success of his mission.[9]

The Ecole Polytechnique became a barracks, or hotel,
for the students in the days and weeks following the
revolution. Classes were suspended indefinitely and the
students had complete freedom to come or go at all hours
of the day and night. General Aupick ordered the cooks
to serve meals around the clock. All pretext of academic
work gave way to service to the new government. Furthermore, the students were to be paid three francs per
day (approximately the wage of an unskilled worker in

Paris) until such time as classes would be resumed.[10] It should be mentioned once again that not all the *polytechniciens* were pleased with the overthrow of the monarchy. Some went home after the revolution, while others remained at the school but took no part in the service to the government or in the general peacekeeping actions of the majority.

The services rendered by the students of the Ecole Polytechnique, and political expediency, caused the Provisional Government to issue a public declaration of gratitude on February 29:

> The Provisional Government, in the name of the Republic, extends its appreciation to the students of the Ecole Polytechnique who, since the first day of the Revolution, put themselves in the service of the Country and who, in all circumstances, gave the most admirable proof of their loyalty by actions, intelligence, and devotion. The Provisional Government hopes that the students of the Ecole Polytechnique will continue their patriotic work.[11]

On February 25 a large column with several pieces of artillery made its way from the Place de la Bastille toward the suburb of Vincennes. At its head were *polytechniciens*. The fortress of Vincennes was the strongest in the vicinity of Paris. It was manned by an adequate garrison well supplied and with ample artillery. It was extremely unlikely that even an armed civilian group such as the one that marched out that morning could have captured the fortress if the troops chose to defend it. Therefore, several of the students rode on ahead of the column to negotiate with the commander of the garrison in order to prevent useless bloodshed. The students were successful. The garrison declared itself in favor of the Republic and pledged its support to the Provisional Government. The gates of the fortress opened and the soldiers fraternized with the people.[12]

The Provisional Government sent *polytechniciens* on missions outside the city. As the revolution spread from Paris in all directions, reports reached the capital of mobs taking the law into their own hands. Several students rushed to Versailles when word was received that the palace was about to be sacked and burned. Upon their arrival they found that several of their comrades, one of whom was A. Henri Resal, future member of the Académie des Sciences and professor at the Ecole Polytechnique. Resal had gone out earlier and, with the aid of students from Saint-Cyr, had gotten the situation well in hand. On February 27 M. Revin, five other *polytechniciens*, and a young military medic were provided with fast horses and sent to Chantilly. Word had been reeceived that the mob was about to burn the famed château. The students arrived in time to prevent any destruction, but the situation was not an easy one as the people sought out symbols of the old order upon which to vent their pent-up frustrations.[13] Other *polytechniciens* accompanied comsssioners of the Provisional Government to cities in the provinces (Rouen, Lyon, Orleans, and so on) to aid in extending the authority of the new regime.

The only *polytechnicien* to be wounded in the February Days did not receive his wound while taking part in revolutionary activities. While walking along the Seine, he was stabbed three times by an unidentified assailant. It appears that there was no connection between the attack and the political events of those turbulent days.[14]

The *polytechniciens* played a limited role in the actual fighting in February. Those who did fight were most often defending barricades although some fought with National Guard units against the insurgents. The neutral role of the majority of the *polytechniciens* was unique, especially on the twenty-fourth, by which time a political polarization had taken place. Their support of the Provisional Government and thus of the Republic did not mean that they were republicans. Rather, they saw in the Provisional Government an instrument of stabilization that could bring an end to the fighting. Their actions did not show a sympathy with the people or with any political cause, but showed, rather, an attempt to control, or manage, the masses so as to restore order. Until the abdication of Louis Philippe they had worked for the restoration of order under the authority of the king; after the abdication they quickly accepted the authority of the Provisional Government and worked equally hard in support of it.

The university students of Paris, and in particular those of the law and medical schools, were not so politically different from the *polytechniciens*. For them the revolution had more meaning—particular goals to be attained. They were concerned about voting rights and the right to assemble, but freedom for the university was utmost in their minds. They deemed the February Revolution a great success, a triumph over the old regime—that is, over the monarchy and its conservative, restrictive policies. For these students the February Revolution was the final victory. In this respect they differed substantially from the working and artisan classes with whom they had allied themselves during the bloody days of fighting.

Whereas the students considered the revolution to be an end in itself, one that resulted in the moderate changes they desired, the working and artisan classes saw the revolution as a means to their ends. The latter sought fundamental social and economic changes that did not enter the minds of the great majority of the bourgeois students. The students were convinced that the Republic would reflect the aims, attitudes, and values of men such as Michelet and Quinet. They were skeptical of socialists such as Louis Blanc and fearful of the radical Auguste Blanqui. The Cabetists and Fourierists had won the loyalty of only a small number of the student population in Paris. The political writings of men such as Michelet and Lamartine were doing much to popularize republicanism, but their brand of republicanism was socially and economically conservative. They looked back to the First Republic, that of the Girondins, as an acceptable political structure. The "good" republic in the eyes of the students was one that would introduce "liberal" political and administrative reform. Thus the honeymoon with the working classes was shortlived. As the weeks and months passed during the spring of 1848, the students and the workers, who had fought side by side in the February Days, parted company. The students, satisfied with the reforms and changes introduced by the bourgeois Republic and content with the National Assembly elected by the people in April, first rallied to the support of the new government and then became less active in political affairs.

The students were given back their "beloved professors" Michelet and Quinet. Both of the suspended teachers resumed their lectures and the students flocked to them in even greater numbers than before.[15] Mickiewicz was not reinstated after the revolution. He was in Italy at the time, but it was his Bonapartism rather than his absence that made the difference. Bonaventure Orfila, dean of the medical school, had been relieved of his duties by the new government shortly after it had taken power, but a sufficient number of students interceded on his behalf and reluctantly the government restored him to the deanship. There was, in those days following the February Revolution, sentiment among the students that deans should be elected by the students of the school over which they presided.[16] However, the idea was not seriously considered by the Ministry of Education or by the university administrators.

An alarming number of people, most of them workers and artisans, hard armed themselves in the course of the three days of fighting. Many of them continued to roam the streets of the capital during the days that followed. With the army's departure from Paris the task of maintaining order fell heavily on the National Guard, the ranks of which were opened to include the lower bourgeoisie, artisans, and even members of the working class. Also formed in these uncertain days was a special battalion of young men, many of whom were students from the various schools of the university, but it was not exclusively a student battalion. *La Lanterne* was indignant when it was referred to as such, and stressed the point that also in its ranks were young men of "commerce" and workers. "What is being called the *battalion of the schools*," it declared, "should be more properly named a Young

Guard."[17] Numbering some six hundred youths, the Young Guard acted as an auxiliary of the National Guard.

The creation of a republic in France introduced a freedom of association that had not been known since the early days of the French Revolution of 1789. No longer were there restrictions on political meetings or organizations. Clubs and societies of every political stripe came quickly into existence. The students of Paris took an active part in a number of these organizations.

The *Club de la Fraternité,* which was founded on the Left Bank, drew from the student population, but neither was it controlled by the students nor was its membership predominantly made up of students. Watripon and his associates exerted the dominant influence on the club and leftist students flocked to the meetings. They were a small percentage of the student population of Paris, but they were the most active. *La Lanterne* became, by its own declaration, the *"Moniteur* of the Club de la Fraternité."[18] The fundamental program of the club was stated to be based upon " 'The Declaration of the Rights of Man and of Citizens' and its practical consequences."[19] Such a broad statement could be interpreted as each individual wished in the early days, but gradually the club moved so far to the left that all but the most radical students dropped from its ranks.

Other organizations formed in these days were the *Société democratique centrale* ("Central Democratic Society") and the *Comité central de election générale* ("Central Committee for the General Election"). The purpose of the former was to "de-mask traitors and to gather together good citizens," whereas that of the latter was to prepare for the forthcoming elections.[20] It was once again the more politically oriented and leftist students who joined these clubs.

The clubs and societies in Paris and in the suburbs, which totaled some two hundred, used every available hall in the city, including those of some schools. The Collège Charlemagne was used by the *Club de l'arsenal* ("Club of the Arsenal"), while the *Société des droits de l'homme* ("Society of the Rights of Man") met at the Ecole des Arts-et-Métiers. The University of Paris opened its amphitheaters to almost a dozen clubs, of which only several had substantial student membership. François Pardigon, a law student, was president of the *Club du deux mars* ("Club of the Second of March"). Other students also served as presidents of various clubs with large student memberships.[21]

Several leading figures of the Paris clubs thought of themselves as students even though they no longer had formal status as such. Napoleon Lebon, forty years of age in 1848, was one of the principal figures of the Society of the Rights of Man. He continued to refer to himself as a medical student although he had quit school in the 1830s to devote his time to what was then a secret society. Joseph Sobrier, active in the club movement and publisher of the left-wing *La Commune de Paris,* had dropped out of law school before completing his studies.[22]

The student committee that had come into existence on the eve of the revolution and that had attempted with very limited success to coordinate and direct student efforts during the February Days continued to function as the Central Committee of the Schools. It now took on the task of coordination and liaison between the schools of Paris and the newly created clubs and societies. With its headquarters at 4, Place de la Sorbonne, the committee received communications every day between the hours of one and four. It maintained ties with various organizations, particularly those on the Left Bank that flourished in the weeks following the revolution when the Provisional Government had neither the means nor the will to control political activities in the capital.

The aftermath of the revolution witnessed a variety of activities on the part of the students. A deputation of students from the Ecole des Beaux-Arts presented itself at the offices of the Provisional Government. They demanded that the state utilize the talents of the graduates of the school to the advantage of the nation rather than to leave them as they had in past years—unemployed.[23] The student deputation was very cordially received at the

Hôtel de Ville. Although the members of the Provisional Government were absent, their staff assured the young men that the government was sympathetic to their problem and would give it serious consideration. The students departed satisfied that their grievance had been heard and, in keeping with the optimism raised by the successful revolution and the creation of the Republic, that favorable action would be taken. But the Provisional Government, acting from weakness in these early days, said yes to almost everyone. As authority and strength were gradually restored through the spring and early summer of 1848 — culminating in the defeat of the workers on the barricades in June — the government ignored demands such as the one made by the Beaux-Arts students. These demands offer one of the clearest indications of dissatisfaction within a segment of the student population as well as an indication of what might be called a surplus of talent in the French capital.

Another deputation of students, this one from the Ecole d'Alfort, went to the Hôtel de Ville to seek the favor of the new government. The students first offered their services and then requested that they be allowed once again to wear swords as they had in the past. The monarchy had deprived them of their swords in 1832 as the result of the students' participation in antigovernment demonstrations. As was at first customary in the Second Republic, the students were granted their wish.[24] A deputation from the Ecole Polytechnique also visited the Provisional Government and asked it to present before the newly elected National Assembly a plan for the reorganization of the Corps des Ponts-et-Chaussées.[25]

L'Avant-Garde, in an article that appears at first glance to have been written with tongue in cheek, asked why all students were not given uniforms. But satire was rarely used in the student-oriented newspapers, and the article must be taken in a more serious vein. The students of the military schools and of the Ecole Polytechnique had fine uniforms, continued *L'Avant-Garde*, why not the law, medical, art, and other students? "At the funeral last Saturday [of M. Salles] the students presented a sorry spectacle" concluded the article. "We will demand the three-cornered hat, sword, and blue uniform, such as that worn by the Ecole Polytechnique, with green trimming and decoration."[26] It is impossible to ascertain how many students were in agreement with such a proposal, but there is no question that the uniforms of the *polytechniciens* were admired by the general population and envied by a portion of the student population.

On March 15 the minister of war ordered the *polytechniciens* to return to school, with the exception of a small number designated by the commanding general to remain in the service of the civil authorities. Upon the return of the students they were immediately given a one-month leave so that they could spend time with their families. Thus it was not until April 15 that the Ecole Polytechnique resumed its regular schedule.[27] Furthermore, on May 5 the minister of war issued an order that exempted the entering class of 1846 from taking the traditional examination for entering public service.[28] This order resulted in the dismissal of the second-year students, leaving only the entering class of 1847 at the school.

The revolution of 1848 was not restricted to Paris, or even to France. It very quickly became a European revolution. In Vienna, Berlin, the lesser German states along the Rhine and the Danube, and Italy,[29] barricades went up and governments were shaken to their foundations. If ever the old maxim "When France sneezes all of Europe catches cold" were true, it was so in 1848. A republic was successfully proclaimed only in France; nevertheless, central Europe was never the same after the upheaval. Furthermore, students frequently participated in these revolutions. In particular, the students were active in Vienna, where the university became a focal point of activity in the spring of 1848. The university communities in the German states, mainly in the south and in the west, were also active in the national and liberal movements of the day.

In Paris the students had a particularly keen feeling for the international aspect of the revolution. They spoke of the German, Austrian, and Italian students as their "brothers" and "comrades." In a letter to the editors of *L'Avant-Garde,* B. Faurax, a law student, wrote, "The cause that has triumphed is not only that of France, but also that of the whole world." Faurax concluded by noting that the struggle was "for the glory of France and all humanity."[30]

In an open letter addressed "To the Students of Germany and Italy," *Comité central des écoles* expressed the general feelings and attitudes of the Parisian students:

Brothers,

With eyes fixed on the painful struggle of Italy and on Germany uneasy and gloomy, the young French Republic, confident in its strength and in the righteousness of its cause, waited.

What would Europe say to France? What would be the response of the kings? It is you who have transmitted the response to us in the name of the people; and it is the most admirable in all of history that brothers have ever made to brothers. You have intoned the hymn of independence, chased the tyrants, broken the thrones and have echoed from one corner of Europe to the other the holy formula of our fathers: Liberty, Equality, Fraternity.

Glory to you, young martyrs of Italy, Vienna, and Berlin. Glory to all of those who bravely fell beneath the bullets of the royalists and cried out with their last breath: Long live Liberty!

You have accomplished an immense task. It is not just Prussia, Austria, or Italy you have freed. It is not only the resurrection of Poland that you have begun. You have signaled the secret hour of the federation of all free people.

Thanks to you, war is no longer possible between the children of the old world; and if a supreme struggle is imminent—that of civilization against barbarism, liberty against despotism—we will stand firmly united by a bond that nothing can destroy. We will march together, with Poland as the advance guard and France on all sides.

Children of Europe, regenerate yourselves, receive the fraternal embrace of young France, which, God willing, will happily fire the cartridges left over from the fighting of February 24 for your defense. Courage—for you struggle on behalf of the universal fraternity.

Long live the Republic![31]

One cannot help but be struck by the international tone
of this letter. It conjures up shades of the great figures of
the First Republic. The men of the 1790s wished to
spread the benefits of the First Republic to the peoples of
the rest of Europe, and Napoleon actually referred to his
campaign of 1807 as the "War of Polish Liberation." The
students' pro-Italian and -Polish feelings are also clearly
apparent. Most significant of all is the conveyed confidence that the February Revolution was a total victory.
The French students no longer needed "the cartridges
left over from the fighting of February 24" because their
goals had been attained. Their principal concern was
"What would Europe say to France? What would be the
response of the kings?"

This same feeling of victory was expressed by an Irish
student studying in Paris: "Permit me, in the name of my
country, poor Ireland, to present to you my congratula-
tions on the occasion of the glorious events that you have
achieved and to assure you that we will never forget the
generous sympathy that you have shown to us. [Signed]
Walsh, Irish Student."[32] The students of Strasbourg and
Tours also expressed their sentiments in glowing words.

Brothers,

We have admired and envied you. While a justifiable and
unanimous insurrection was taking place in Paris against a
villainous government and an antinational dynasty you were
placed on the front rank. Brothers separated by distance, but
one in feelings, we were able only to participate by shouts of
liberty, honor, glory, and triumph to you combatants!

Sons of the Heroes of '93, men of the revolution of 1848, be
proud to have contributed by shedding your blood for the
revival of the nation. Unite our hands and our hearts in the
triple symbol of liberty, equality, and fraternity![33]

From Strasbourg:

Brothers and friends!

You have displayed the dignity of your fathers of '89 and
1830. Born of a glorious revolution, a perjurious government

weighed heavily upon France! After it had taken away all rights, it had dared to curb freedom of thought; you have nobly protested. Glory to you for having done so! Furthermore, you took an active part when the people took to the streets to bring the traitor to justice. You entered the struggle only after being assured of your motto: Liberty! Equality! Fraternity!—Long live the nation! The deputies of the German universities have just arrived and they sign this document with us.[34]

The students of the provinces not only were envious of their Parisian counterparts: they seem also to have felt cheated out of playing what they considered to be an important role in the making of history. Liberty, equality, and fraternity—of the 1789 variety—appeared to them to have been won on the barricades. Their tone also reassured the students in the capital of the complete success of the February Revolution.

On June 1, 1848, the students of Paris held a large banquet for a delegation of visiting Viennese students. The honored guests were members of the famed Academic Legion, which had been created in Vienna in March following the early successes of the revolution in the Austrian capital. The Academic Legion was originally made up of students and professors of the University of Vienna. Then its ranks were opened to alumni, and before the Legion was dissolved the membership included some rather dubious "students." But in June, when the Austrian students arrived in Paris, the Legion was riding the crest of its popularity, and for many students throughout Europe it provided an example of student power and influence. The Legion patrolled the streets of Veinna, posted guards at the city's gates, and protected the university. The relationship between the students and the workers was one of trust and good feeling, thus enabling the Legion to maintain peace and order in Vienna.

On the Thursday afternoon designated for the banquet some three hundred students gathered in the Place du Panthéon and marched to the large salon of Constant-Voinot at the barrier (or city limits, at each point of which a toll gate stood) of Montparnasse. Here, with citizen Hippolyte Carnot, minister of public education, presiding, the Viennese students were honored and praised for their role in the Austrian revolution, but at the same time the banquet took even more of an international flavor. After the speeches, which were led off by Carnot himself, toasts were made, as at the prerevolutionary banquets, by representatives of the various schools of Paris: Polytechnique, Normal, Saint-Cyr, Central, Val-de-Grace, d'Alfort, and the faculties of medicine and law. The general theme of the toasts was a call for unity and brotherhood among the students of the world. Sympathy was repeatedly proclaimed for the oppressed Polish people.[35]

Elections were held on April 23 for a National Assembly, which was charged with the task of drawing up a constitution for the Republic and of governing the country until such time as the new republican institutions became operative. The elections, held nationwide, quite naturally reflected the views of France — not just of Paris, the seat of the revolution. In the capital the bourgeoisie were generally satisfied with the conservative make-up of the Assembly. Alexis de Tocqueville, forever an aristocrat, wrote contemptuously of the large number of inexperienced deputies: "I am convinced that nine hundred English or American peasants, picked at random, would have better represented the appearance of a great political body."[36] The artisan and working classes viewed the new National Assembly with alarm and dismay. Its bourgeois make-up looked too much like that of the old Chamber of Deputies. What had the revolution been all about? Louis Philippe was gone and Guizot was gone, but little had changed; even less might be expected from the Assembly, which did not represent their political, economic, or social aspirations. On May 15, the occasion of a debate on Poland, the workers of Paris marched on the Palais-Bourbon, disrupted the meeting of the Assembly and, more as an afterthought than as part of a preconceived plan, made a half-hearted attempt to overthrow the Provisional Government.

The drums were beaten and the National Guard
turned out in strength. It remained loyal to the government and with a minimum of fighting restored order. It
all happened so quickly and unexpectedly that the students of Paris were hardly involved. Word that a mob had
invaded the Assembly and had declared it dissolved
reached the Ecole Polytechnique at three o'clock in the
afternoon. General Jean Victor Poncelet, the new commander of the school, convened the students of the second division (the entering class of 1846 had already been
dismissed) in the amphitheater and announced that the
National Assembly had been attacked by a seditious mob.
Then as he launched into a political speech the students
interrupted him and demanded that they march to the
aid of the government. In full uniform the *polytechniciens*
made their way once again through the streets of the
Latin Quarter. In the vicinity of the Palais du Luxembourg they were met by a staff officer of the National
Guard who informed them that the situation was well in
hand at the Palais-Bourbon and who suggested that the
students go instead to the Luxembourg and form a guard
for the president of the Assembly, who had sought refuge there during the upheaval. This the students did,
and for the next three days they performed the duties of
a special guard detachment at the Luxembourg. On May
18 they were instructed to return to their school, as the
danger had passed and as their services were no longer
needed.[37]

L'Avant-Garde wrote that, besides the *polytechnicien* students, students from the Ecole Normale and the *jeunesse
des écoles* also went to the aid of the National Assembly. It
congratulated these students for their vigilance, but at
the same time lamented the apathy into which Parisian
students as a whole had lapsed. The students, declared
the newspaper, had formed the *avant-garde* of the revolution, and it singled out their demonstration of February 3
and alluded to their participation in the February Days.
However, it continued, since the victory had been
achieved they had lost a great part of their *ardeur: La
Lanterne* no longer appeared—it was not published in

April—and only *L'Avant-Garde* remained; the revolution was over but there were still present real and imminent dangers to the Republic. *L'Avant-Garde* saw these dangers coming from both the Right and the Left. It called upon the National Assembly to act against the "instigators of disorder and anarchy" for "without order no society is possible." It asserted that freedom was not possible so long as the government permitted license; the government should have long ago closed certain clubs and disbanded committees that were potential threats. "It is easier to conquer than it is to make good use of the victory," it concluded, "easier to acquire than to conserve." *L'Avant-Garde* thus made a new appeal to youth and to the students in particular. Once again it was time to defend the nation. May 15 would not be an isolated incident; there would be more like it and the students must be prepared. They must organize themselves for the defense of the Republic as they did in the days before February 24 for a confrontation with the power of the monarchy.[38]

As the spring of 1848 advanced, however, the political activities of the students declined. The Provisional Government had granted them most of their desires in the weeks following the February Days. The election and convening of the National Assembly satisfied their political aspirations. As for the future, it would be in the hands of the representatives of the people and the students seemed to have complete faith in the Republic. If there were apprehensions on the part of a few, clearly the vast majority had indeed lost their *ardeur*. "Apathetic" may be too strong a term to describe the students of that spring; "satisfied" may be more appropriate. The comité central des écoles no longer functioned; the Young Corps no longer functioned; the students had returned to their lectures and books.

As the students became less and less active through the spring of 1848, the workers became more so. Neither the Luxembourg Commission headed by Louis Blanc nor the national workshops nor the other minor concessions made by the new government satisfied the aspirations of the workers. They wanted meaningful social and economic reform but the new regime, bourgeois in nature, had no more intention of complying with their demands than had the monarchy. Demonstrations in March, April, and May served only to widen the gap between the workers and the government. The workers, whose leaders had been arrested after May 15, felt that they were once again being deprived of the fruits of victory. It was a repetition of the events of 1830. They had fought on the barricades and had overthrown the oppressive July Monarchy only to have it replaced by an equally unsympathetic, bourgeois Republic. When the national workshops were closed on June 21, they saw only one course of action left open to them—barricades!

On June 22 the workers and artisans[39] assembled at the Panthéon, marched to the Place de la Bastille, where they paused for a moment of silence, and then set about the grim task of building barricades. Never before had they believed that they had so much to gain. The July Revolution of 1830 and the February Revolution of 1848 had taught them that one had merely to dominate Paris to overthrow the existing government and to replace it with another of one's choice. This time victory would not slip through their fingers. A social democracy would be created under the direct supervision of the workers and artisans, and the new government would usher in the millenium.

The problem that confronted the "people of June" was that most of France, and in particular the rest of Paris, feared their victory even more than the disaffected desired it. The Parisian bourgeoisie thus turned out en masse when the drums were beaten. Troops were used in a much wiser manner than they had been in February and proved to be more loyal. There was much more at stake for all concerned in June than there had been in February or in 1830, and the bitterness of the fighting and the increased casualties reflected the hatred that had built up on both sides of the barricades.

The students' role and influence in the June Days was relatively insignificant. Few students sympathized with the cause of the workers and even fewer fought with them on the barricades. The vast majority supported the National Assembly in spirit if not in deed. As the academic year had ended, most of the students had gone home by the time the fighting broke out. They had never championed social or economic reform and now generally shared the same conservative concept of the Republic as that held by the National Assembly. Thus there was no broad-based student movement, only the isolated actions of individual students who either lived in Paris or happened to have remained in the capital.

When the fighting broke out in June, the president of the Assembly, Antoine M. Sénard, sent orders to the Ecole Polytechnique for the students to come to the Palais-Bourbon to protect the representatives of the people. There were only thirty-six students still living at the school. The first division, it will be recalled, had been excused from classes and examinations in May as a token of gratitude for their role in the February Revolution. Then on June 11 General Eugène Cavaignac, who had been given extraordinary powers to govern as the air of crisis mounted, had visited the school. He found the students of the second division restless, distracted, and generally unable to settle down to serious studying. Therefore, he had suggested that classes be accelerated, examinations be given early, and the studens be sent home.

On June 23 the thirty-six *polytechniciens* who remained dressed in full uniform and marched out through the huge front gate into the predominately working-class section of Paris. Despite the students' cries of "Down with the traitors!" the insurgents did not interfere with their passage. When they arrived at the Palais-Bourbon they were greeted by M. Senard, who shook the hand of each student. For three days and three nights they bivouacked in the Palais-Bourbon and performed a variety of menial, noncombat tasks such as carrying messages about the city and standing guard duty in and around the Palais-Bourbon. Frustrated and bored, the students began to drift off one or two at a time to see firsthand what was taking place in the combat sections of the city or to play an active role in the fighting.

On June 23 two *polytechniciens*, MM. Fargue and Bobillier, attached themselves to the Seventh Battalion of the Mobile Guard and assisted in the attack on barricades in the rues du Faubourg-Poissonnière and de Lafayette. In the course of the very heavy fighting Bobillier was wounded slightly in the leg.[40] Unable to return to the school that night because the district was in the hands of the insurgents, Fargue slept at an army post on the Left Bank. The next morning he assisted in the capture of the Place Maubert.

When Fargue arrived before the barricade that extended across the rue Montagne-Sainte-Geneviève, fighting had not yet broken out. One of the insurgents, recognizing his uniform, accused him of treason and reminded him of the not too distant past when the *polytechniciens* were on the side of the people. "It is still that way," Fargue replied. "You are not the people and we do not want barricades raised against the Republic and the National Assembly!" The insurgent then pointed out to the student that there were six hundred royalists in the Assembly and that the insurgents objected to this type of republic. Fargue answered that he did not agree with that statement and, declaring that he was the enemy of the barricade defender, he shouted "Long live the National Assembly!"[41] This cry signaled the beginning of the battle. A soldier standing next to Fargue was immediately struck by a musket ball and the student was taken prisoner. Fargue was confined to a room at 64, rue de la Montagne-Sainte-Geneviève, from which he was later rescued by soldiers and taken to the Ecole Polytechnique.

In the course of the June Days students of the Ecole Polytechnique who had earlier departed from Paris returned to take an active part in opposing the insurrection. Furthermore, former *polytechniciens*, wearing as much of their old uniforms as they could find, fought on the side of the Assembly. One of these young men, Louis Lesbros, the son of Colonel Lesbros, second in command of the Ecole Polytechnique, was killed in the fighting.

Young Lesbros had completed his studies at the Ecole
Polytechnique in June, 1847, and was attending the Ecole
des Mines. When the fighting began he put on his old
uniform and joined a volunteer unit of the National
Guard. While attacking one of the barricades that
formed the defensive network of the Place Maubert, he
was struck in the shoulder by a musket ball. Taken to a
nearby first-aid station opposite 39, rue des Noyers, he
was treated by M. Corlieu, a fourth-year medical student.
He was then taken to his home at 7, rue Corneille, where
his family watched over him until he died on July 24,
1848. Lesbros was buried in the cemetery of Montparnasse (section one of the seventeenth division), which was
reserved for graduates of the Ecole Polytechnique. En-
graved on the column that marks his resting place is the
following inscription:

A LEUR CAMARADE

C.-J.-B.-L. LESBROS

élève ingenieur des mines, ancien élève de l'école
polytechnique
mort d'une blessure reçue le 24 juin 1848
en combattant pour l'ordre et la liberté

———————————

LES ÉLÈVES DE L'ÉCOLE POLYTECHNIQUE[42]

Vaneau, the *polytechnicien* who was killed in the attack
upon the military barracks in the rue de Babylone in the
July Revolution of 1830, is buried near Lesbros. However, the hero of 1830 has received more favorable
treatment than his fallen comrade. Not only has a street
in the vicinity been named after Vaneau, but each year
since 1830 a deputation of students from the school
places a wreath on his grave. M. Corlieu, the medical
student who had administered first aid to Lesbros, was to
write of Lesbros in later years: "The same death merits
the same commemoration."[43]

Corlieu was attached to the hospital clinic of the faculty
of medicine in Paris when the June Days began. He was
also a member of the Eighth Company of the Twelfth
Legion of the National Guard. On June 23 he served with

his company at the Palais-Bourbon, but on the morning of the twenty-fourth, after attending mass at the church of the Madeleine, he found himself on the Right Bank with the fighting getting heavy. He placed himself at the disposal of Dr. Ricque, who was in charge of a first-aid center at the Palais Bonne-Nouvelle (in the district of Ménagère), and was put to work at once as the wounded began to arrive. Corlieu spent the entire afternoon caring for the wounded. When all had been attended, he sought to make his way back to the Latin Quarter. After reaching the Left Bank, he was caught in a cross fire between insurgents and government troops, and found himself, quite by accident, in the hands of the insurgents. Recognized by members of his National Guard company who were defending the barricades, he was put to work caring for the wounded insurgents. An attack by government troops captured the first-aid station in which he was working, and he again found himself in the service of the government.[44]

On June 25 Corlieu moved his wounded to the hospital clinic of the faculty of medicine and resumed his duties there. On the twenty-sixth he was put in personal charge of the care of General Martin de Bourgon, who had been wounded in heavy fighting. Despite all that could be done, the general died. On the morning of the twenty-seventh, Corlieu visited briefly with his father, who was serving with the National Guard unit from Charly which had come to Paris to support the government. Young Corlieu then returned to the hospital clinic and his duties.[45] He supported the government and the National Assembly in the June struggle, but his political feelings, which were not strong, gave way to his humanitarian feelings and, no doubt, the persuasiveness of armed men when he found himself among the insurgents. He worked to save lives, whether of insurgents or of soldiers.

M. Levasseur, a graduate of the Collège Bourbon, was a *pensionnaire* of the Institut Boutet. During the June Days he served in the Ninth Legion of the National Guard, as his parents lived in the rue de la Victoire. He was shot in the course of the fighting, but the musket ball hit the sturdy leather of his equipment and he escaped injury.[46]

The students of the Collège Louis-le-Grand were, as might be expected from their generally bourgeois origins, sympathetic towards the government and the National Assembly. The vast majority took no part in the events of June. They were confined to their school and they remained there. Fighting took place in the streets about the school, however, and one insurgent even fought from the roof of the school.[47] Henri Dabot, a student at Louis-le-Grand, wrote to his parents on Sunday, June 25: "Yesterday, Saturday, the fighting continued. We knew all morning that there were soldiers in the rue Saint-Jacques who had not eaten since noon of the previous day. We gave them our lunch and were pleased that we could make that small contribution for the *Patrie*."[48]

At least one student from Louis-de-Grand fought during the June Days. Dabot told his parents that this young man served with the Mobile Guard and that, when his lieutenant was wounded in combat and he brought him to the infirmary, he was surrounded by his fellow classmates, who embraced him, shook his hand, and praised his actions.[49] Several students from the Collège Descartes fought side by side with their fathers.

In the aftermath of the June Days the government's forces arrested 11,642 "insurgents." Included in this number were 40 who gave their occupation as "student." However, in the first screening of the prisoners, 30 students were released because there was no real evidence that they had acted as insurgents. Many of those released were medical students who had been caring for the wounded of both sides. Most of the remaining 10 were either deported from France (to French colonies) or given light prison terms.[50] Reynard, who was arrested on June 25, spent six weeks in La Force prison. The young man was released after his father appealed to the government to consider his own service in the revolution of 1830 and his son's in February, 1848. Although Reynard returned to his study of law in the fall, the untimely death

Conclusion

The students of Paris were not revolutionaries in 1848, they were reformers. They had grievances that revolved primarily around problems within the academic community although they shared some of the political grievances, both domestic and foreign, of the nation at large. The changes they desired were not of a social or an economic nature, and the students were not, with the exception of a very small minority, "radicals" in the contemporary sense of the term. The frustrations of January and February, 1848, were vented in demonstrations that took place during those months and that culminated in their actions on February 22. It was on that day that the students made their most significant contribution to the revolution. Their participation, example, and leadership on February 22 were instrumental in directing and sustaining the demonstration that led the Parisian population to rise up against a government it wished to reform. As the reform movement of February 22 and 23 became the revolution of February 24, the students continued to participate, but their influence on the course of events became less in the overall picture.

Student participation was not an essential ingredient on February 24, as it had been on February 22. Once the momentum of the insurrection increased with working-class participation, student participation, which also increased in terms of numbers, became less critical to the ultimate outcome. Nevertheless, students of the Ecole Polytechnique played a significant role in reducing the

amount of bloodshed on February 24 by their intervention at various key points throughout the city. Furthermore, the medical students were influential in reducing
suffering and saved many lives by their diligent care of
the wounded in hospitals, in first-aid stations, and at the
barricades. But the question is whether a revolution
would have taken place at all in February, 1848, had not
the students played a leading role on February 22. The
dynastic opposition had never intended to violate the law
and quickly drew back when the banquet was prohibited
by the government. The organizing committee for the
banquet canceled the affair on the night of February 21
and was prepared to submit to a parliamentary debate
and to some form of legal confrontation. The crowd that
gathered before the church of the Madeleine on the
morning of February 22 was unorganized and
peaceful—until the arrival of the students and their allies. Clearly, the catalyst that sparked the demonstration
and that led to the construction of barricades and to
bloodshed was provided by the students and the young
men of the Latin Quarter. This is not to say that the
students had planned a revolution. Their aims on that
fateful day had been protest and demonstration. They
had undertaken such actions on various occasions in the
past. Yet it was their indispensable contribution that led
to revolution.

The concessions made to the academic community and
the constitutional reforms enacted and implied by the
new regime were sufficient to satisfy the students. They
were convinced that the revolution had been a success.
The National Assembly, which met in the spring, was
composed of conservative republicans and liberal
monarchists. It received the approval and support of the
students. When the workers and artisans of Paris began
to display hostility toward the Provisional Government
and the National Assembly, the students were unsympathetic. They did not take part in the antigovernment
demonstrations in April and May, and they did not support the social or economic demands of the lower classes.
During the June Days the students tended to refrain

from taking an active part in the fighting. What student participation there was, was limited and on an individual basis. There was no student movement. The students were in sympathy with the limited changes brought about by the February Days, but when a genuine revolution threatened — one that would drastically change the political, social, and economic structures of France — the students of Paris did not give it their support.

Notes

Introduction

1. Richard Rush to James Buchanan, No. 6, Paris, September 24, 1847, Unpublished Diplomatic Dispatches, State Department Archives, Dispatches, France. National Archives, Washington, D.C.

2. As quoted in Priscilla Robertson, *Revolutions of 1848,* p. 17.

3. As quoted in Daniel Stern, *Historie de la révolution de 1848,* vol. 1, p. 28.

4. Richard Rush to James Buchanan, No. 18, Paris, March 14, 1848, State Department Archives, Dispatches, France.

5. Alexis de Tocqueville, *Recollections,* trans. Alexander Teixeira de Mattos, pp. 29–30.

6. In his *Recollections* Tocqueville gives the date of this speech as January 30. However, the speech appears in *Le Moniteur Universel,* the semiofficial organ of the government, on January 28 and the text indicates that it had been delivered the previous day. See editor's note, ibid., p. 16*n*5.

7. Ibid., pp. 16–19. The complete text of this speech may be found in George Lawrence's translation of the complete works of Tocqueville, pp. 722–30.

I. Background for a Revolution

1. See Félix Ponteil, *Histoire de l'enseignement en France,* pp. 157–221; Louis Trénard, "L'Enseignement secondaire sous la monarchie de juillet, pp. 81–133; Paul Gerbod, *La Condition universitaire en France au XIXᵉ siècle,* pp. 27–140; and Antoine Prost, *L'Enseignement en France, 1800–1967,* pp. 147–206.

2. On the Collège Louis-le-Grand see Gustave Dupont-Ferrier, *Du Collège de Clermont au Lycée Louis-le-Grand, 1563–1920;* and R. R. Palmer, ed., *The School of the French Revolution.*

3. See Erwin H. Ackerknecht's excellent work, *Medicine at the Paris Hospital: 1794–1848,* pp. 31–44.

4. Amable Longepied, one of the founders of the Club of the Revolution following the February Days, had prepared himself to become a science teacher during the July Monarchy. Peter Amann writes that he "had probably been blacklisted by the state-sponsored secondary schools" for his political views and activities; *Revolution and Mass Democracy: The Paris Club Movement in 1848,* pp. 131–32.

5. Paul Gerbod, *La vie quotidienne,* p. 48.

6. Ibid., p. 40.

7. Only 6.3 percent of the teachers in 1914 had fathers who were professors; see ibid., p. 40.

8. See "Law on the Formation of an Imperial University," in Palmer, ed., pp. 222–29.

9. Gerbod, *La vie quotidienne,* pp. 106–9; and Trénard, L'Enseignement secondaire sous la monarchie de juillet, pp. 85–87.

10. [Albert Dresden Vandam], *An Englishman in Paris,* pp. 27–28.

11. Ibid., pp. 2–3.

12. Ibid., pp. 29–30.

13. Charles Godfrey Leland, *Memoirs,* p. 17.

14. Ibid.

15. "Modernized" refers to an increase in the sciences and, in the last quarter of the century, the social sciences, while the study of the classics, in particular Latin and Greek, declined. On educational reform under the July Monarchy see Trénard, "L'Enseignement secondaire sous la monarch de juillet.

16. See Edgar Quinet's autobiography, *Edgar Quinet avant l'exil,* pp. 318–417.

17. *La Lanterne du Quartier Latin* 2, no. 1 (January, 1848).

18. Ibid.

19. Archives Nationales (hereafter AN), BB[18] 1455; Archives de la Préfecture de Police (Paris), two reports dated December 28, 1847, and January 5, 1848; and *La Lanterne,* ibid.

20. *La Lanterne,* ibid.

21. Ibid., 1, no. 2 (February, 1847).

22. Accounts of this affair were carried in both *La Réforme* and *Le National* (February 23, 1847), and in *La Lanterne* 1, no. 3 (March, 1847).

23. See "Vive l'Italie" and "Volontaires pour l'Italie," *La Lanterne* 1 no. 9 (September, 1847).

24. Ibid., 1, no. 6 (June, 1847).

25. Virtually every issue of *La Lanterne* in 1847 (twelve in all) had one or more articles dealing with Polish, Italian, or Irish repression and attacks upon the respective dominating power.

26. *La Lanterne* 1, no. 9 (September, 1847).

27. Ibid., 1, no. 4 (April, 1847).

28. See John J. Baughman, "The French Banquet Campaign of 1847–48," pp. 1–15.

29. *La Lanterne* 1, no. 7 (July, 1847).

30. Ibid., 1, no. 9 (September, 1847).

31. Ibid., 1, no. 11 (November, 1847).

32. AN, BB^{30} 296, Deposition Roinville; and Lepelletier Roinville, *Histoire du banquet réformiste,* p. 10.

33. Ibid.

34. *La Réforme, Le National,* and so on (January 5, 1848).

35. *La Lanterne* 2, no. 1 (January, 1848).

36. For an account of the events of January 6, see ibid.

37. In a letter to the minister of public instruction dated February 7, 1848, Gabriel Delessert, prefect of police for the city of Paris, states that Watripon was a "former student"; Archives de la Seine, 4AZ 1100.

38. AN, BB^{18} 1460, G. Delessert to the minister of justice, February 16, 1848,

39. Both journals maintained a high level of quality in their reporting of events. Their accounts of student demonstrations before the February Revolution and of student activities during and following the revolution are often borne out by contemporary newspapers and memoires. They are seldom contradicted.

40. AN, BB^{18} 1460, G. Delessert to the minister of justice, February 16, 1848; see also AN, BB^{18} 1460, two brief letters from the Bureau of Criminal Affairs of the Ministry of Justice dated February 29, 1848 (signatures illegible).

41. Archives de la Seine, 4AZ, 1100, Gabriel Delessert to minister of public instruction, February 7, 1848.

42. Ibid.; and *L'Avant-Garde* 1, no. 2 (February, 1848).

43. As given in *L'Avant-Garde,* ibid.

44. Ibid.

45. AN, BB^{18} 1460, M. le Procureur Général to M. le Garde des Sceaux, February 19, 1848.

46. Ibid.

47. AN, BB^{18} 1460, letter from the Ministry of Justice to the Préfecture de Police (Paris), February 22, 1848.

48. See Lucien de Le Hodde, *Histoire des sociétés secrètes et du parti républicain de 1830 à 1848,* p. 415; and Roinville, p. 34.

49. Roinville, p. 11.

50. See David H. Pinkney, *The French Revolution of 1830,* pp. 270, 355–56.

51. *La Lanterne* 1, no. 7 (July, 1847).

52. Ibid.

53. See Jean Tulard, *La Préfecture de Police sous la Monarchie de juillet,* pp. 105–13.

54. Ibid.

II. The Making of a Rebellion:
February 22 and 23

1. Percy B. St. John, *French Revolution in 1848*, p. 108. St. John was living in Paris in the rue Saint-Honoré during the February Days. His eyewitness account of the events was written during the spring immediately following the revolution.

2. *La Lanterne du Quartier Latin* 2, no. 3 (March, 1848).

3. Lepelletier Roinville, *Histoire du banquet réformiste*, pp. 38–39.

4. Archives de la Préfecture de Police (Paris), *Distribution des Récompenses Nationales*, Aa 372, Dossier Bellan; and Aa 380, Dossier Commelin.

5. *Le Moniteur Universel* (February 23, 1848).

6. *La Lanterne* 2, no. 3 (March, 1848).

7. AN, F^{1}D III 89, Claude L. Giubega's statement to the Commission des blessés de février 1848.

8. See Philippe Faure, *Journal d'un combattant de février*, p. 134.

9. Ibid., p. 131.

10. Ibid., p. 133.

11. As quoted in St. John, p. 110.

12. Faure, p. 134.

13. Ibid. See also AN, F^{1}D ··· 86, Dossier Debock.

14. AN, BB^{30} 296, Deposition Lemoine-Tascherat, no. 283.

15. AN, BB^{30} 296, Procès-verbal from the Quartier des Champs-Elysées, signed by Joseph-Gabriel Pollomy.

16. AN, F^{1}D ··· 89, Dossier Guibega.

17. *La Lanterne* 2, no. 3 (March, 1848).

18. See Archives de la Préfecture de Police (Paris), Aa 380, Dossier Commelin.

19. See ibid., Aa 372, Dossier Bellan.

20. See ibid., Aa 380, Dossier Corlieu.

21. *La Lanterne* 2, no. 3 (March, 1848).

22. See AN, BB^{30} 296, G. Delessert, Préfect de police, "Raport sur les événements de 1848."

23. Archives de l'Ecole Polytechnique, *Registre Matricule des Elèves*, vol. 8, *1846–54*.

24. As quoted in Jean-Pierre Callot, *Histoire de l'Ecole Polytechnique*, p. 29.

25. See G. Pinet, *Histoire de l'Ecole Polytechnique*, pp. 159–60; and Callot, ibid., pp. 68–69. David H. Pinkney (*The French Revolution of 1830*) minimizes the role of the students in the July Revolution. Of the students of the Ecole Polytechnique he writes, "Had the combatants depended on the students of the Ecole Polytechnique for leadership they surely would have been

defeated, for few if any of the students appeared on the scene until the twenty-ninth"; and, "Of the 250 or more Polytechnicians who sympathized with the opposition to Charles X only sixty-one actually fought in the July Days and those only on the final day after the outcome was largely decided" (pp. 269–70).

26. Callot, p. 72.

27. Ibid., p. 80.

28. On the "Dubois Affair" see six letters that deal with it in the Archives de l'Ecole Polytechnique, 1848; and *La Gazette de France* (January 31, 1848).

29. See C. J. Madeleine Loir, unpublished manuscript, p. 3. Loir was a second-year student at the Ecole Polytechnique and took an active part in the events of February, 1848. See also AN, F¹ᴅ ⋯ 91, Dossier Walery; Jean Walery was with the student demonstrators outside the Ecole Polytechnique. See also Pinet, p. 238.

30. AN, BB³⁰ 297, Procès-verbal du quartier Saint-Jacques.

31. Henri Dabot, *Lettres d'un lycéen et d'un etudiant de 1847–54,* p. 5.

32. *Le Siècle* (February 24, 1848).

33. AN, BB³⁰ 297, Deposition Lavocat.

34. Ibid.

35. Loir, p. 4; and *La Lanterne* 2, no. 3 (March, 1848).

36. Archives de l'Ecole Polytechnique, 1848, "Notes sur les événements qui se sont passées à l'Ecole Polytechnique depuis février 1848 jusqu'en 1854," p. 2; and Loir, p. 5.

37. Ibid.

38. On the activities of the students of the Ecole Polytechnique see AN, BB³⁰ 296, General Aupick's report to the king dated 9:30 A.M, February 24, 1848. See also Pinet, pp. 237–40; Callot, pp. 81–84; and Colonel Mourral, *Charles de Freycinet,* p. 10.

39. *La Lanterne* 2, no. 3 (March, 1848).

40. AN, BB³⁰ 297, Procès-verbal du quartier du Jardin des Plantes, no. 230; and *La Lanterne* 2, no. 3 (March, 1848).

41. Charles Godfrey Leland, *Memoirs,* p. 179.

42. AN, F¹ᴅ ⋯ 85, Dossier Canada.

43. AN, F¹ᴅ ⋯ 85, Dossier Carrère.

44. Archives de la Préfecture de Police (Paris), Aa 372, Dossier Bellan.

45. Ibid., Aa 380, Dossier Commelin.

46. Levasseur, "Souvenirs d'un collégien en 1848," p. 4.

47. See *L'Avant-Garde* 1, no. 5 (March, 1848).

48. *La Lanterne* 2, no. 3 (March, 1848).

49. Edgar Quinet, *Edgar Quinet avant l'exil,* p. 396.

50. AN, BB³⁰ 296, Procès-verbal du quartier du Luxembourg, no. 222.

III. The Rebellion Becomes a Revolution:
February 24

1. Albert Crémieux, *La Révolution de février,* p. 217.
2. AN, BB³⁰ 297, Deposition Brunet, no. 683.
3. Leland stayed at the hotel de Luxembourg in the rue de la Harpe. This resident house had the reputation of being "a nest of rather doubtful and desperate characters"; Charles Godfrey Leland, *Memoirs,* p. 172–73.
4. Ibid., p. 179.
5. *La Lanterne du Quartier Latin* 2, no. 2 (March, 1848).
6. AN, BB³⁰ 297, Deposition Roinville, no. 10; and *La Lanterne,* ibid.
7. Ibid.
8. AN, BB³⁰ 297, Deposition Lavocat.
9. Ibid.
10. AN, BB³⁰ 297, Deposition Roinville, no. 10.
11. AN, BB³⁰ 297, General Aupick to the minister of war, February 24, 1848; and C. J. Madeleine Loir, Unpublished manuscript, pp. 10–11.
12. Loir, pp. 11–12; and AN, BB³⁰ 297, Deposition de Lestre, no. 8.
13. As quoted in G. Pinet, *Histoire de l'Ecole Polytechnique,* p. 243.
14. Colonel Mourral, *Charles de Freycinet,* pp. 12–13.
15. Wilfried de Fonvielle, "L'Ecole Polytechnique au 24 février 1848," p. 821.
16. AN, BB³⁰ 297, Deposition Pasteur d'Etreillis.
17. AN, BB³⁰ 297, Deposition Jourdan, no. 477.
18. AN, BB³⁰ 296, Deposition Gaseuel.
19. Pinet, p. 244.
20. *La Lanterne* 2, no. 2 (March, 1848).
21. AN, BB³⁰ 297, Deposition Roinville, no. 10.
22. A number of accounts deal with the events outside the Ecole Polytechnique: AN, BB³⁰ 297, Procès-verbal du quartier du Jardin des Plantes, no. 230; idem, Deposition Guyot, no. 793; idem, Deposition Plendoux, no. 794; idem, Deposition Beaulaincourt, no. 798; idem, Deposition Calonne, no. 803; idem, Deposition Grattier, no. 804; and Archives de l'Ecole Polytechnique, 1848 "Notes sur les événements qui se sont passées à l'Ecole Polytechnique depuis février 1848 jusqui'ou 1854," pp. 4–5.
23. Pinet, p. 244.
24. AN, BB³⁰ 297, Procès-verbal du quartier du Jardin des Plantes.
25. Archives de l'Ecole Polytechnique, 1848, "Notes sur les

événements qui se sont passées à l'Ecole Polytechnique depuis février 1848 jusqui'ou 1854," pp. 4–5.

26. AN, F¹D⋯ 96, Dossier Robin; and idem, BB³⁰ 296, Deposition Gobert, no. 11.

27. Pinet, p. 243.

28. See Fonvielle, p. 823.

29. AN, F¹D⋯ 91, Dossier Jacquier. There are three documents in Jacquier's file: two are letters from Jacquier dated April 24, 1848, and December, 1849; the third is an unsigned statement giving the vital facts on Jacquier dated January, 1850.

30. AN, F¹D⋯ 96, Dossier Reynard: and idem, BB³⁰ 296, Police report, no. 220.

31. Archives de la Préfecture de Police (Paris), Aa 414, Dossier Stoffel.

32. Ibid., Aa 410, Dossier Remy.

33. Ibid., Dossier Redon.

34. Ibid., Aa 380, Dossier Corlieu.

35. AN, BB³⁰ 296, no. 220, Police report from the Sorbonne quarter.

36. Ibid.

37. AN, F¹D⋯ 89, Dossier Guerreau.

38. Archives de la Préfecture de Police (Paris), Aa 415, Dossier Ubel.

39. Ibid., Aa 391, Dossier Greppo; and idem, Aa 374, Dossier Boussard.

40. Ibid., Aa 401, Dossier Henri A. Martin.

41. Ibid., Aa 400, Dossier Manin.

42. AN, F¹D⋯ 96, Dossier Raincourt.

43. Aa 391, Dossier Guigard.

44. AN, BB³⁰ 297, Procès-verbal du quartier de l'Observatories, no. 228; and *La Lanterne* 2, no. 2 (March, 1848).

45. Archives de l'Ecole Polytechnique, 1848, "Notes sur les événements qui se sont passées à l'Ecole Polytechnique depuis février 1848 jusqui'ou 1854," p. 2.

46. Percy B. St. John, *French Revolution in 1848,* p. 288.

47. Maxime Du Camp. *Souvenirs de l'armée 1848,* p. 101.

48. Loir, pp. 15–16.

IV. The Students and the Provisional Government

1. Charles Godfrey Leland, *Memoirs,* p. 180.

2. Colonel Mourral, *Charles de Freycinet,* p. 14; and G. Pinet, Histoire de l'Ecole Polytechnique, p. 249.

3. *L'Avant-Garde* 1, no. 3 (March, 1848).

4. *Le Moniteur Universel* (March 1, 1848).

5. C. J. Madeleine, Loir, Unpublished manuscript, p. 23.

6. Pinet, p. 254.

7. Ibid.

8. *Le Moniteur* (February 26, 1848).

9. Loir, p. 23.

10. Archives de l'Ecole Polytechnique, 1848, Melcion d'Arc to M. Lefebores, February 28, 1848.

11. *Le Moniteur* (February 29, 1848). The two student newspapers, *La Lanterne* and *L'Avant-Garde,* refused to print the government's statement of appreciation because they felt that the students of the Ecole Polytechnique had not fully supported the revolution.

12. Percy B. St. John, *French Revolution in 1848,* pp. 235–36.

13. Pinet, p. 253.

14. *L'Ami du Peuple* (February 27, 1848).

15. See *La Lanterne* 2, no. 3 (March, 1848).

16. See ibid.

17. Ibid.

18. Ibid.

19. Ibid.

20. *L'Avant-Garde* 1, no. 5 (March, 1848).

21. Peter Amann, *Revolution and Mass Democracy,* p. 58.

22. Amann writes that 5 percent of the club presidents whose names he could find were students. This would be about eight or nine students; see ibid., p. 41.

23. *L'Avant-Garde* 1, no. 3 (March, 1848).

24. Ibid.

25. *Procès-verbaux du gouvernment provisoire et de la commission du pouvoir executif: 24 février–22 juin 1848* [April 17, 1848] (Paris: Archives Nationales, n.d.).

26. *L'Avant-Garde* 1, no. 5 (March, 1848).

27. Archives de l'Ecole Polytechnique, 1848, "Conseil de Perfectionnement de 1832 à 1850," Séance du 20 Mars 1848.

28. Ibid., Séance du 19 mai 1848.

29. Rebellions had taken place in the Italian states before February 22, but it was the news from Paris that set into motion the revolution of 1848 south of the Alps.

30. *L'Avant-Garde* 1, no. 5 (March, 1848).

31. Ibid.

32. Ibid., no. 3 (March, 1848).

33. Ibid.

34. *La Lanterne* 2, no. 3 (March, 1848).

35. *L'Avant-Garde* 1, no. 8 (June, 1848).

36. Alexis de Tocqueville, *Recollections,* p. 111.

37. *L'Avant-Garde* 1, no. 7 (May 1848); and Pinet, pp. 263–64. For a full account of the events of May 15, see Peter Amann, "A *Journée* in the Making: May 15, 1848," pp. 42–69.

38. *L'Avant-Garde* 1, no. 7 (May, 1848).

39. Roger Price gives a very good account of just who were

the "workers" of June, 1848. His statistical evaluation of 11,642 insurgents who were arrested following the collapse of the insurrection indicates that they were workers, artisans, and *petite bourgeoisie;* see *The French Second Republic: A Social History,* pp. 163–71.

40. Pinet, p. 269.

41. Ibid.

42. Corlieu, *Les Journées de juin 1848,* pp. 5–7.

43. Ibid.

44. Ibid.

45. Ibid.

46. Levasseur, "Souvenirs d'un collégien en 1848."

47. Henri Dabot, *Lettres d'un lycéen et d'un étudiant de 1847 à 1854,* pp. 30–31.

48. Ibid.

49. Ibid.

50. AN, F[7] 2585. For a full discussion and analysis of the 11,642 arrested following the collapse of the insurrection see Price, pp. 162–80; and Charles Tilly and Lynn H. Lees, "The People of June, 1848," pp. 174–202.

51. AN, F[1]D III 96, Dossier Reynard.

52. AN, F[1]D III 91, Dossier Jacquier.

Bibliography

Archives

The following archives in Paris were the most helpful in the preparation of this study:

Archives National
Archives de l'Ecole Polytechnique
Archives de la Préfecture de Police (Paris)
Archives de la Seine

Of particular interest at the Archives Nationales were the three cartons of deposition (BB^{30} 296–98) taken from principal participants. These provided several hundred eyewitness accounts that have not found their way into print. The dossiers of those wounded in the fighting (F^{1D}··· 84–98) were also of great value, as were many other scattered materials. The Archives de l'Ecole Polytechnique provided good information on the students and the school in 1848. The major finds here were the two unpublished manuscripts "Notes sur les événements qui se sont passées à l'Ecole Polytechnique de 1848 à 1855" (unsigned), and C. J. Madeleine Loir's account of his role in the February Days. In the archives of the Paris police are forty-seven cartons of dossiers entitled *Distribution des Récompenses Nationales* (Aa 370–417). The majority of these dossiers are from February, 1848. The remainder are related to the revolution of 1830 and to the insurrections of 1832 and 1834. The diplomatic dispatches of Richard Rush, housed in the National Archives, Washington, D.C., were also consulted.

Journals

L'Ami du Peuple
L'Avant-Garde
Le Commerce

Le Courrier Français
La Démocratie Pacifique
La Gazette de France
Gazette des écoles
Journal des écoles
La Lanterne du Quartier Latin
Le Moniteur Universel
Le National
La Patrie
La Réforme
Le Siècle
L'Union Monarchique

Two journals were significantly more useful than the others. *La Lanterne du Quartier Latin* and *L'Avant-Garde* both served as student newspapers. Their principal editors were not, in 1848, students, but students served on their editorial staffs. Their articles were for and about the academic community of Paris. Published once a month, they were widely read by the students—and by the police. *La Lanterne* was first published in January, 1847, and appeared monthly through March, 1848. It was not published in April, May, or June of 1848. *L'Avant-Garde* made its debut in the Latin Quarter in January, 1848. It published three issues in March, following the February Revolution, and then monthly through June, 1848.

Books and Articles

Ackerknecht, Erwin H. *Medicine at the Paris Hospital: 1794–1848.* Baltimore: Johns Hopkins Press, 1967.
Actes de congrès historique du centenaire de la révolution de 1848. Introduction by R. Fawtier. Paris: N.p. 1948.

Agulhon, Maurice. *1848, ou l'Apprentissage de la république, 1848–1852.* Paris: Editions du Seuil, 1973.
Les Quarante-huitards. Paris: Editions Gallimard/Julliard, 1975.
Alméras, Henri d'. *La vie parisienne sous la république de 1848.* Paris: A. Michel, n.d.
Alton-Shée, Edmond Count of. *Souvenirs de 1847 et de 1848.* Paris: M. Dreyfous, 1879.
Amann, Peter. "A *Journée* in the Making: May 15, 1848." *Journal of Modern History* 42 (March, 1970): 42–69.
———. *Revolution and Mass Democracy: The Paris Club Movement in 1848.* Princeton: Princeton University Press, 1975.
Barrot, Odilon. *Mémoires.* 4 vols. Paris: Charpentier, 1875–76.
Baughman, John J. "The French Banquet Campaign of 1847–48." *Journal of Modern History* 31 (March, 1959), 1–15.

Blanc, Louis. *1848: Historical Revelations*. London: Chapman and Hill, 1858.

Bonde, Baroness Florence. *Paris in 1848*. New York: James Pott and Co., 1903.

Boucher, Henri. *Souvenirs d'un parisien pendant la second république*. Paris: Perrin, 1908.

Boudart, René. *L'Organisation de l'Université et de l'enseignement secondaire dans l'Académie impériale Gênes entre 1805 et 1814*. Paris: Mouton et Cie, 1962.

Cabet, Etienne. *Bien et mal, danger et salut après la révolution de février 1848*. Paris: P. Martinon, 1849.

Cahen, Georges. "Louis Blanc et la Commission du Luxembourg." *Annales de l'école libre des sciences politiques*. Vol. 12. Paris: N.p., 1897.

Callot, Jean-Pierre. *Histoire de l'Ecole Polytechnique ses légends, ses traditions, sa gloire*. Paris: Les Presses Modernes, n.d.

Caron, P. "Cabet et l'Icarie en 1847." *Revue d'histoire moderne et contemparaine* 12 (1907).

Carr, E. H. *The Romantic Exiles: A Nineteenth-Century Portrait Gallery*. New York: Frederick A. Stokes, 1933.

Castéra, Noël. *Le Triomphe de la liberté, ou histoire la plus complete de la révolution de 22, 23, et 24 février*. Paris: Robert, 1848.

Castéra, Noël. *La Vérité sur le préfecture de police pendant l'administration de Caussidière*. Paris: Palais-National, 1850.

Caussidière, Marc. *Mémoires de M. Caussidière, ex-préfect de police et représentant du peuple*. 2 vols. Paris: Michel Lévy Frères, 1849.

Caute, David. *The Left in Europe since 1789*. New York: McGraw-Hill, 1966.

Chapman, Brian, and Chapman, Joan Margaret. *The Life and Times of Baron Haussmann*. London: Weidenfeld and Nicolson, 1957.

Chenu, Adolphe. *Les conspirateurs: Les sociétés secrètes la préfecture de police sous Caussidière*. Paris: Garnier Frères, 1850.

Collins, Irene. *The Government and the Newspaper Press in France, 1814-81*. London: Oxford University Press, 1959.

———. *Government and Society in France, 1814-1848*. New York: St. Martin's Press, 1970.

Corlieu. *Les Journées de juin 1848*. Extracted from *L'Echo républicain de l'Aisne*, June 22, 24, and 27, 1888.

Coutin, André. *Huit siècles de violence au quartier latin*. Paris: Stock, 1969.

Crémieux, Albert. *La Révolution de février; étude critique sur les journées de 21, 22, 23 et 24 février 1848*. Paris: E. Cornély, 1912.

Daumard, Adeline. *La Bourgeoisie parisienne de 1815 à 1848*. Paris: S.E.V.P.E.N., 1963.

Dabot, Henri. *Letters d'un lycéen et d'un étudiant de 1847 à 1854*. Paris: Blériot et Gautier, n.d.

Delbrouck, E. *22, 23, et 24 février. Révolution de 1848 et événements qui l'ont causée.* Paris: Tous les Marchands de Nouveautés, 1848.

Delmas, Gaëtan. *Curiosités révolutionnaires. Les journaux rouges: Histoire critique de tous les journaux ultra-républicaines publiées à Paris depuis le 24 février jusqu'au 1er octobre 1848.* Paris: Bureau Central, 1848.

de Luna, Frederick A. *The French Republic under Cavaignac, 1848.* Princeton: Princeton University Press, 1969.

Documents pour servir à l'histoire de nos moeurs: Manuscrit de février 1848. Paris, 1868.

Dommanget, Maurice. *La Révolution de 1848 et le drapeau rouge.* Paris: Spartacus, 1948.

——. *Auguste Blanque, des origines à la révolution de 1848: Premiers combat et premières prisons.* Paris: Mouton et Cie, 1969.

Du Camp, Maxime. *Souvenirs de l'année 1848.* Paris: Hachette, 1892.

Dumas, Alexandre (père). *Révélations sur l'arrestation d'Emil Thamas.* Paris: Michel Lévy Frères, 1848.

Dupont-Ferrier, Gustave. *Du Collège de Clermont au Lycée Louis-le-Grand, 1563–1920.* 3 vols. Paris: M. Munier, 1921–25.

Duveau, Georges. *1848: The Making of a Revolution.* Translated by Anne Carter. New York: Random House, 1967.

Falloux, Alfred-Frédéric-Pierre de. *Mémoires d'un royaliste.* Paris: Perrin, 1888.

Faure, Philippe. *Journal d'un combattant de février.* Jersey: C. Le Feuvre, 1850.

——. "Un journaliste de 1848." *Bulletin de la société d'histoire de la révolution de 1848* 3 (1906–7).

Flotard. "Le 24 février 1848 à l'hôtel de ville de Paris." *Revue Hebdomadaire* 8, 2d series (1901).

Fonvielle, Wilfried de. "L'Ecole Polytechnique au 24 février 1848." *Revue politique et litteraire: Revue bleue* 9, 4th series (1898).

[Un Garde National.] *Journées de la révolution de 1848.* Paris: Louis Janet, n.d.

Garnier-Pagès, Louis Antoine. *Histoire de la révolution de 1848.* 10 vols. Paris: Société du Patriote, 1860–71.

Gerbod, Paul. *La Condition universitaire en France au XIXe siècle.* Paris: Presses Universitaires de France, 1965.

——. "La Vie universitaire à Paris sous la restauration." *Revue d'histoire moderne et contemporaine* 13 (janvier–mars, 1966), 5–48.

——. *La vie quotidienne dans les lycées et colleges au XIXe siècle.* Paris: Hachette, 1968.

Godechot, Jacques. *Les Révolutions de 1848.* Paris: Editions Albin Michel, 1971.

Gorce, Pierre de la. *Histoire de la seconde république française.* 2 vols. Paris: E. Plon, Nourrit et Cie, 1887.

Gossez, R. *Les ouviers de Paris. Vol. I: L'organisation (1848–51).* La Roche-sur-Yon: Centrale de l'ouest, 1967.

Groiseilliez, François de. *Histoire de la chute de Louis Philippe.* Paris: N.p., 1851.

Guillemin, Henri. *La première résurrection de la République 24 février 1848.* Paris: Gallimard, 1967.

Guyon, L. "Un journaliste de 1848." *La Révolution de 1848* 3 (Novembre–décembre, 1906).

Heine, Heinrich. *French Affairs: Letters from Paris.* Translated by Charles G. Leland. 2 vols. London: W. Heenemann, 1893.

Higgonnet, Patrick L.-R., and Higgonnet, Trevor B. "Class, Corruption and Politics in the French Chamber of Deputies, 1846–1848." *French Historical Studies* 5 (Fall, 1967), 204–24.

Ibos, Pierre Emile Marius. *Le Général Cavignac, un dictateur républicain.* Paris: Hachette, 1930.

Johnson, Douglas W. *Guizot: Aspects of French History, 1787–1874.* Toronto: University of Toronto Press, 1963.

[L., countess of.] *Manuscrit de février 1848.* Paris: Emile Voitelain et Cie, 1868.

Lamartine, Alphonse de. *History of the French Revolution of 1848.* Translated by Francis Durivage and William S. Chases. Boston: Phillips, Sampson and Co., 1849.

Lamayre, Gérard Noël. *Haussman "Préfect de Paris."* Paris: Flammorion, 1958.

Latouche, A. *Pages de philosophie de l'histoire sur la révolution de 1848.* Paris: N.p., 1852.

Lavisse, Ernest. *L'Etudiant.* Paris: Calmann Lévy, 1899.

Le Hodde, Lucien de. *Histoire de sociétés secrètes et de parti républicain de 1830 à 1848.* Paris: Lanier et Cie, 1850.

———. *La Naissance de la république en février 1848.* Paris: Chez l'Editeur, 1850.

Leland, Charles Godfrey. *Memoirs.* New York: D. Appleton and Co., 1893.

Lemoine, Edouard. *Abdication du roi Louis Philippe recontée par lui-même.* Paris: Michel Lévy Frères, 1951.

Levasseur. "Souvenirs d'un collégien en 1848." *La Révolution de 1848.* Vol. 2 (1905).

Loir, C. J. Madeleine. Unpublished manuscript, dated March 27, 1848. Archives de l'Ecole Polytechnique, 1848.

Marnay, A. J. de. *Mémoires secrets et témoignages authentiques.* Paris: Librairie des bibliophiles, Paris: 1875

Marriott, J. A. R. *The French Revolution of 1848 in its Economic Aspect.* Oxford: Clarendon Press, 1913.

Marvel, Ik. [Donald G. Mitchell] *The Battle Summer: Being Transcripts from Personal Observation in Paris during the Year 1848.* New York: Baker and Scribner, 1850.

Marx, Karl. *The Class Struggles in France (1848-1850)*. New York: International Publishers, 1964.

McKay, Donald C. *The National Workshops: A Study in the French Revolution of 1848*. Cambridge: Harvard University Press, 1933.

Michelet, Jules. *Journal*. Vol. 1. *1828-1848*. Paris: Gallimard, 1959.

————. *The People*. Translated by John P. McKay. Urbana: University of Illinois Press, 1973.

Monchanin, A. *1848 Histoire de la révolution de 1848*. Paris: Paul Ollendorff, 1887.

Mourral, Colonel. *Charles de Freycinet et l'Ecole Polytechnique en 1848*. Grenoble: Allier Père et Fils, 1937.

Normanby, C. H. P. Marquis of. *A Year of Revolution from a Journal Kept in Paris in 1848*. 2 vols. London: Longman, Brown, Green Longman and Roberts, 1857.

Nougarede, Auguste. *La Vérité sur la révolution de février 1848*. Paris: Amiot, 1950.

Ortega y Gasset, Jose. *The Revolt of the Masses*. New York: W. W. Norton and Co., 1957.

Palmer, R. R. *The School of the French Revolution: A Documentary History of the College of Louis-le-Grand and its Director, Jean-François Champagne, 1762-1814*. Princeton: Princeton University Press, 1975.

Pardigon, François. *Episodes des journées de juin 1848*. London: Jeffs, 1852.

Pelletan, Eugène. *Histoire des trois journées de février 1848*. Paris: L. Colas, 1848.

La Presse ouvrière, 1819-1850. Edited by Jacques Godechot. Paris: Bibliothèque de la révolution de 1848, 1966.

Pinet, G. *Histoire de l'Ecole Polytechnique*. Paris: Librairie Polytechnique Baudry et Cie, 1887.

Pinkney, David H. *The French Revolution of 1830*. Princeton: Princeton University Press, 1958.

Ponteil, Félix. *Histoire de l'enseignement en France*. Paris: Sirey, 1966.

Powers, Richard H. *Edgar Quinet: A Study in French Patriotism*. Dallas: Southern Methodist University Press, 1957.

Price, Roger. *The French Second Republic: A Social History*. New York: Cornell University Press, 1972.

Proces-verbaux du gouvernment provisoire et de la commission du pouvoir executif: 24 février-22 juin 1848. Paris: Archives Nationales, n.d.

Proudhon, Pierre Joseph. *Les Confessions d'un révolutionnaire pour servi à l'histoire de la révolution de février*. Paris: Au bureau du journal "La Voix du Peuple," 1850.

Prost. Antoine. *Histoire de l'enseignement en France, 1800-1967*. Paris: Armand Colin, 1968.

Quentin-Bauchart, Pierre. *La Crise sociale de 1848*. Paris: N.p., 1920.

Quinet, Edgar. *Edgar Quinet avant l'exil*. Paris: N.p., 1888.

Regnault, Elias. *Histoire de huit ans, 1840–1848*. Paris: Pagnerre, 1852.

Richomme, Charles. *Journées de l'insurrection de juin, 1848, par un garde national, précédées des murs de Paris, journal de la rue, collection des principales affiches opposées de février à juin, 1848*. Paris: N.p., 1848.

Robertson, Priscilla. *Revolutions of 1848: A Social History*. Princeton: Princeton University Press, 1952.

Roinville, Lepelletier. *Histoire du banquet réformiste du XIIe arrondissement, depuis sa fondation, le 5 décembre 1847 jusqu'au 24 février 1848*. Paris: Plon Frères, 1848.

Rothfels, Hans. "1848: One Hundred Years After." *Journal of Modern History* 20, no. 4 (December, 1948), 291–319.

Rude, George. *The Crowd in History: A Study of Popular Disturbances in France and England, 1730–1848*. New York: John Wiley and Sons, 1964.

Rush, Richard. *Occasional Productions Including a Glance at the Court and Government of Louis Philippe and the French Revolution of 1848, while the Author Resided as Minister from the United States at Paris*. Philadelphia: Lippincott and Co., 1860.

——. Unpublished Diplomatic Dispatches. State Department Archives, Dispatches, France. National Archives, Washington, D.C.

Saint-Amant, Imbert de. *Le Drame des Tuileries après la révolution du 24 février, 1848*. Paris: N.p., 1848.

St. John, Percy B. *French Revolution in 1848: The Three Days of February, 1848*. London: Bentley, 1848.

Sarrans, B. *Histoire de la révolution de février 1848*. Paris: A l'Administration de Librairie, 1851.

Seignobos, Charles. *La Révolution de 1848. Le Second empire*. Paris: Hachette, 1921.

Sigmann, Jean. *1848 Les Révolutions romantiques et démocratiques de l'Europe*. Paris: Calmann-Levy, 1970.

Spitzer, Alan B. *The Revolutionary Theories of Louis Auguste Blanqui*. New York: Columbia University Press, 1957.

Stern, Daniel [Marie, comtesse d'Agoult]. *Histoire de la révolution de 1848*. 3 vols. Paris: G. Sandré, 1868.

Thomas, Emile. *Histoire des ateliers nationaux*. Paris: Michel Lévy, Frères, 1848.

Thureau-Danquin, P. *Histoire de la monarchie de juillet*. 7 vols. Paris: E. Plon, Nourrit et Cie, 1884–92.

Tilly, Charles, and Lees, Lynn H. "The People of June, 1848." In *Revolution and Reaction: 1848 and the Second French Republic*, edited by Roger Price. New York: Barnes and Noble, 1975.

Tocqueville, Alexis de. *Recollections*. Translated by George

Lawrence. Edited by J. P. Mayer and A. P. Ker. New York: Anchor Books, 1971.

Trénard, Louis. "Agitation universitaire sous Louis Philippe: Quinet et Lenormant." *Le Bugey,* October, 1954.

————. "L'Enseignement secondaire sous la monarchie de juillet: Les Réformes de Salvandy." *Revue d'histoire moderne et contemporaine* 12 (Avril–juin, 1965), 81–133.

Tulard, Jean. *La Préfecture de Police sous la Monarchie de juille suivi d'un inventaire sommaire et d'extraits des Rapports de la Préfecture de Police consérves aux Archives Nationales.* Paris: Imprimerie Municipale, 1964.

Watripon, Antonio. *Histoire politique des écoles et des étudiants, 1814–1848.* Paris: P. Martinon, 1849.

Whitridge, Arnold. *Men in Crisis: The Revolution of 1848.* New York: Charles Scribner's Sons, 1949.

[Vandam, Albert Dresden.] *An Englishman in Paris: Notes and Recollections.* Vol. 1. *Reign of Louis Philippe.* New York: D. Appleton and Co., 1892.

Véron, Louis. *Mémoires d'un bourgeois de Paris.* 6 vols. Paris: G. de Gonet, 1853–55.

Index